InfoTrac College Edition Workbook

for

Crooks and Baur's

Our Sexuality

Ninth Edition

Paz Galupo
Towson University

THOMSON

WADSWORTH

Australia • Canada • Mexico • Singapore • Spain • United Kingdom • United States

Printed in the United States of America
1 2 3 4 5 6 7   07 06 05 04

Printer: Globus Printing

0-534-63383-8

For more information about our products, contact us at:
Thomson Learning Academic Resource Center
1-800-423-0563

For permission to use material from this text or product, submit a request online at
http://www.thomsonrights.com
Any additional questions about permissions can be submitted at
thomsonrights@thomson.com

Thomson Wadsworth
10 Davis Drive
Belmont, CA 94002-3098
USA

Asia
Thomson Learning
5 Shenton Way #01-01
UIC Building
Singapore 068808

Australia/New Zealand
Thomson Learning
102 Dodds Street
Southbank, Victoria 3006
Australia

Canada
Nelson
1120 Birchmount Road
Toronto, Ontario M1K 5G4
Canada

Europe/Middle East/South Africa
Thomson Learning
High Holborn House
50/51 Bedford Row
London WC1R 4LR
United Kingdom

Latin America
Thomson Learning
Seneca, 53
Colonia Polanco
11560 Mexico D.F.
Mexico

Spain/Portugal
Paraninfo
Calle/Magallanes, 25
28015 Madrid, Spain

Table of Contents

Preface

InfoTrac Users Guide

Preface

Welcome to the InfoTrac Workbook, a companion to Crooks & Baur's textbook, *Our Sexuality*. This guide encourages you to apply critical and analytic thinking skills to the information provided in your textbook. For each chapter of the text, this workbook includes nine to thirteen exercises that are designed specifically to use the information available on the InfoTrac online database.

It is easy to get into and use InfoTrac. The InfoTrac pass code is included with your textbook. Instructions for performing InfoTrac searchers are in the User Guide, which can be found online at the InfoTrac web address. They are also included here.

Many of the exercises in this guide suggest search terms that will help you locate articles on the subject at hand. Those **search terms** will appear in bold. Some exercises require you to determine the search terms yourself. Check the User Guide frequently for search tips and suggestions for ways to refine your search. Once you are familiar with InfoTrac, you will discover that there are a number of ways to find information on a given subject.

It is important to approach the information you find on InfoTrac just as you would any resource – with a critical eye. Keep in mind the following:

Consider the source.
Not all sources are equal in quality. Some are "peer-reviewed," meaning that several experts who remain anonymous to the author read the article and agreed it was worth publishing. That does not mean they necessarily agree with the article or its methods and findings. What it does mean is that they believe the article makes a contribution to the discussion about a certain topic or to a field of study.

Peer-reviewed journals in the field of Human Sexuality include *The Journal of Sex Research, Archives of Sexual Behavior, Journal of the History of Sexuality*, and many others. Remember that even peer-reviewed articles need to be judged on their merit. Take into account the author's qualifications, the methods used, and the theoretical approach. You may want to review the information in Chapter 2 of your texts on the strengths and weaknesses of the various types of sex research.

InfoTrac also includes articles from population magazines and other sources that do not send articles out for peer review. Read them with the same critical eye you apply to the academic journals. Depending on their quality, these sources may be perfectly valid and valuable material for your research.

Consider the perspective or approach.
All research and writing takes a particular stand or approach to a problem or question. An article on how people form sexual relations, for example, may be viewed from a psychological perspective in one journal, a historical one in another, and from that of evolutionary biology in a third. Learn to recognize the different approaches and become familiar with the assumptions that accompany these and other perspectives.

Some exercises focus on a subject that may be either controversial or has recently received a lot attention. For these, use the most recent articles you can find because the information on the topic may be changing rapidly.

In addition to reading the InfoTrac articles, the exercises in this guide may ask you to do your own fieldwork or to assess you own experience or opinion. Try to incorporate your own findings and observations with the InfoTrac research sources.

I hope that you enjoy the research and analytic process and that these exercises help deepen your understanding of human sexuality.

About the Author

M. Paz Galupo, Ph.D. is an Associate Professor of Psychology at Towson University. Her teaching and research interests include human sexuality related to sexual orientation identity.

QUICK START GUIDE

InfoTrac College Edition, a complete Online Research and Learning Center, contains over 10 million full-text articles from nearly 5,000 scholarly and popular periodicals. Covering a broad spectrum of disciplines and topics, this online library is ideal for every type of research. *InfoTrac College Edition's* articles are updated daily and include research dating back to 1980. In addition to the database, *InfoTrac College Edition* offers InfoWrite, a web-based training tool designed to help develop writing skills. InfoWrite assists students through difficult areas of research writing, such as choosing a topic, composing introductions and conclusions, and crediting sources.

Registration

Step 1
Go to www.infotrac-college.com and click on **Register New Account.**

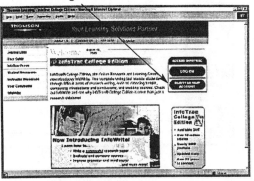

Step 2
Enter passcode and create a username.

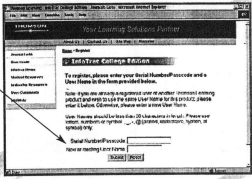

Step 3
Fill out the registration form completely to activate your account.

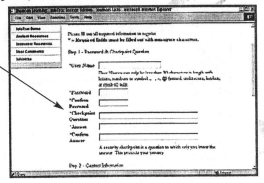

Note: After registration is complete, you will only need your <u>username and password</u> to logon.

USING INFOTRAC COLLEGE EDITION

There are three types of searches:

- Subject Guide Search
- Keyword Search
- Advanced Search

Subject Guide Search

Step 1

Type in the term(s) you would like to search and click Search.

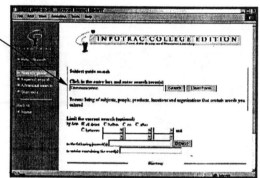

Step 2

After a list of results appear, select an article by clicking on the title. If your search words do not match the Subject Guide database, a list of similar and related subjects will appear. Simply select the subject that most closely matches your topic.

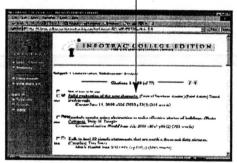
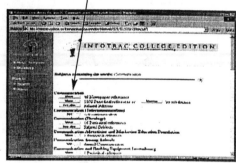

Step 4

A list containing bibliographic information for each article in your search to a maximum of 20 articles per page. To view an article, click on the citation.

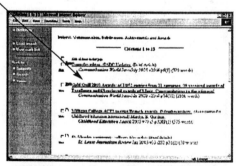

If the term(s) you typed in the **Subject Guide** cannot be found, it will automatically default to the **Keyword Search.**

Keyword Search

The **Keyword Search** looks for the word or words entered. It is more effective when looking for a specific topic, title, author, or product.

Search by **Keyword** just as you would by **Subject Guide**.

The search will return with a list of articles containing the keyword term(s). Results are listed from most recent to oldest publication date.

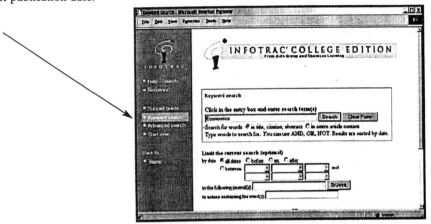

Advanced Search

With **Advanced Search**, a more specific search can be conducted.

Step 1
Select an index to search by. What is an index? Each article is indexed by certain variables. These indices include the title, author, publication's name, where and when it was published (see the list on the next page). Type your search criteria in the entry box to the right.

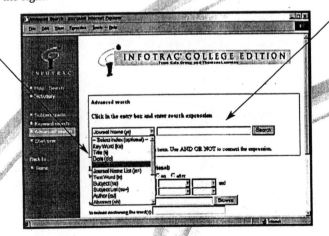

Step 2
If you want to search by multiple criterion, simply repeat the process with an operator between them.

- Logical operators(and/or/not) specify inclusive or exclusive relationships between search terms or result sets.
- Proximity operators (Wn, Nn) specify that two search terms must be within a specific distance (in words) of each other. Proximity operators work only with free text indexes such as keywords, abstracts, text, and titles.
- Range operators (since, before, etc.) specify upper bounds, lower bounds or both searches for numeric data. Numeric indexes include publication dates, number of employees and annual sales.

Indexes for Advanced Search

Abstract (ab): Includes words from article abstracts as well as from any author's abstracts.

Author (au): Authors are indexed in surname/given name order; for example, "nelan bruce w." It's best to search in surname-first order. Enter a surname and, optionally, a given name.

Date (da): The date the article was published.

Journal Name (jn): The name of the magazine or periodical.

Journal Name List (jn=): Provides a list of magazines or periodicals in which the search term appears.

Keyword (ke): Words in article titles and authors, as well as subjects, people, companies, products, vocations, events, etc., featured in articles.

Record Number (rn): A full record always includes a unique record number. If you note a record number, you can easily find the record again with the record number index.

Refereed (re): Experts in the same field as the writer review articles in the journal and ensure that the data and methodology has met a high standard. This is also knows as a peer reviewed.

Source (so): Lets you search for records by the type of source from which they're taken (e.g., magazine, journal, or newspapers).

Source List (so=): Lets you browse a list of subjects that contain the word or words you type.

Subject (su): Lets you search for references by the source types under which they are indexed.

Subject List (su=): Provides a list of references by source types.

Text Word (tx): Composed of all words from the body of articles.

Title (ti): The title index is composed of all words in the article.

Volume Number (vo): The volume of the magazine or periodical.

Using Wildcards in the Advanced Search

At times, you might want to find more than just exact matches to a search term. For instance, you might want to find both the singular and plural forms of a word or variant spellings. Wildcards let you broaden your searches to match a pattern.

InfoTrac provides three wildcards:

- An asterisk (*) stands for any number of characters, including none. For example pigment* matches "pigment," "pigments," "pigmentation," etc. The asterisk wildcard can also be used inside a word. For example, colo*r matches both "color" and "colour."
- A question mark (?) stands for exactly one character. Multiple question marks in a row stand for the same number of characters as there are question marks. For example, psych????y matches either "psychology" or "psychiatry", but not "psychotherapy."
- An exclamation point (!) stands for one or no characters. For example, analog!! matches "analog," "analogs" or "analogue" but not "analogous."

If you see a message about a search being invalid, you'll need to add at least one character before one of the wildcards.

Mark List

Clicking on the **Mark Box** allows you to select articles you would like to retrieve for later viewing. The **Mark Box** is available in two ways:

1. While viewing the citation list, you may select individual articles or you may select all the items on the page.

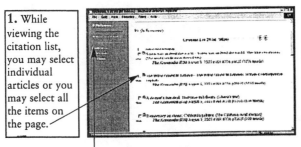

2. Check the **Mark Box** while you are in article view.

Click on **View Mark List** to view selected articles.

Limit Search

You may limit your search if you find yourself immersed in citations or of the citations are too general. Limit your search to dates, specific journals, and keywords. The **Limit Search** function is available in two ways:

*1. Limit a search that has already been performed. To do this, click on **Limit Search** in the left navigation.*

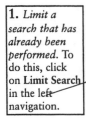
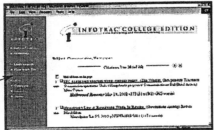

2. Limit a current search. To do this, fill out the Limit Search box below the search field.

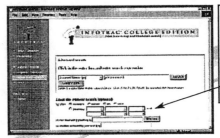

Article Retrieval

There are three article retrieval options available:

* **Browser Print:** Print out the full text article
* **Acrobat Reader:** Review article as a PDF file
* **Email Delivery:** E-mail article to self or others

Click on **Print or Email** on the left navigation bar while viewing citations.

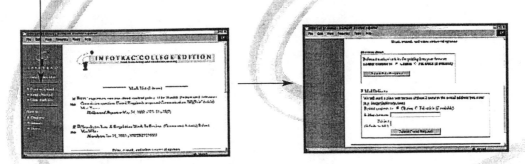

Chapter 1

Perspectives on Sexuality

1.   Sexuality and Diversity: Where do you fit in?

Using InfoTrac, look up **sexuality and diversity, sexual diversity,** or simply **sexuality**. Find and read an article that best exemplifies your perspective and/or experience related to sexuality.

     a.   What about the article speaks to you as an individual?

     b.   What more would you like to learn about this topic?

Find and read an article related to sexuality that represents a very different perspective and/or experience from your own.

     c.   What about this article interests you?

     d.   What more would you like to learn and understand about this topic?

2.   Sexuality and Controversy: Where do you stand?

Using InfoTrac, look up **sexuality and controversy**. Choose and read articles for one controversial issue and then answer the following questions.

     a.   What is the nature of the controversy?

     b.   How do individuals on each side of the issue characterize the opposing side?

     c.   Where do you stand on the issue? What informs your position?

     d.   Thinking about someone who might take a different view on this controversy, how might his or her experiences be similar to or different from your own?

3. Sex Education: How Do We Learn About Sex?

How did you learn about sex? Was your greatest source of information your parents, your friends, teachers, books, the Internet, or other media?

Compare your experience with what researchers have discovered about how people become informed about sex.

Using InfoTrac, look up **sex education**. Choose one source of sex information such as the Internet, parents, health class, etc., and evaluate its quality.

     a.   What are the advantages of this source?

     b.   What are its disadvantages?

What do you think about restricting sex education courses to **abstinence** education? Examine at least two sources based on studies of this "just say no" approach to sex.

     c.   What are the advantages of abstinence education?

     d.   What are its disadvantages?

4. Sex Education Across the Lifespan

Often sex education is a topic that is discussed in the context of adolescence. Use InfoTrac to explore the ways in which individuals continue to learn about sex and sexuality across the lifespan. Are the sources the same as when you were a teenager? Examine at least two sources on **adult sexuality, sexuality and midlife,** or **sexuality and aging**.

     a.   How is sexuality discussed similarly or differently across different life stages?

     b.   What issues were discussed that are more relevant to you now than when you were first learning about sex and sexuality?

5.   *Psychosocial Orientation*

The textbook states that it views sexuality using a psychosocial orientation.   This approach emphasizes that psychological factors (emotions, attitudes, motivations) and social conditioning impact our sexual attitudes, values, and behavior. Using InfoTrac, search key terms **psychosocial orientation and sexuality**. Briefly skim 3-4 articles and answer the following questions:

      a.   In what ways do the articles exemplify the psychosocial approach to understanding sexuality?

      b.   What factors specifically do the articles identify as impacting sexuality?

      c.   In what ways would your understanding of the topic change if a psychosocial approach had not been taken?

6.   *Religion and Sex*

Religion plays a powerful role in regulating sexuality and influencing how we think about and experience sex. Each topic has a history in the Judeo-Christian tradition and remains significant today.

Choose <u>one</u> of the following topics:
        Celibacy
        Madonna/Whore (or Mary/Eve) dichotomy
        Virginity
        Sex as sinful
        Adam and Eve
        Pro-Creation

Using InfoTrac, find out:
- The origin of the concept or story
- Its impact on male and female sexuality
- How the idea has changed over time
- Its status today

Give one example that shows the presence or absence of your chosen theme in contemporary culture.

7. Consider the Research: Is there Still a Sexual Double Standard?

Is the **double standard** a thing of the past? Read the introduction and discussion sections of "Does the Sexual Double Standard Still Exist? Perceptions of University Women" by Robin R. Milhausen and Edward S. Herold in the *Journal of Sex Research*, November 1999. Note especially the discussion of the "reverse double standard."

Compare your observations to the issues raised in this article.

      a.   Do we still expect more conservative sexual behavior from women than from men?

      b.   Are notions such as "virgin" and "slut" still used only to label women? What terms are used to characterize the sexuality of men?

      c.   Are there signs that the double standard has changed or lessened? If so, to what do you attribute this change?

Also consider:

      d.   How do same-sex relations fit into the double standard? Has greater acceptance of non-heterosexual relations helped to change sex and gender stereotypes?

8. Sex in Mass Media

Music videos sell CDs but, according to their critics, they also sell a version of sex that objectifies women. Other observers claim that commercial film and television programs with explicit sex have negative effects on young people.

What do you think about the way sex appears in media? Using InfoTrac, search articles using key terms **sex and mass media** to examine studies of one specific medium (TV, radio, film, video, the Internet, print advertising, or MTV). Then answer the following questions:

      a.   Have depictions of sex in this medium become more explicit over time? Is that impression substantiated by research?

      b.   Does the medium sexualize men as well as women? How are the depictions of men and women similar and different?

      c.   Are safer sex practices ever mentioned or shown? If so, how are they portrayed?

d. Do you think there should be restrictions on the sexual topics shown or discussed in mass media? If so, who should impose those restrictions? What are the drawbacks to such censorship?

9. *Consider the Research: What Do Magazines Teach Us About Sex?*

Using InfoTrac, locate the article "From Girls into Women: Scripts for Sexuality and Romance in Seventeen Magazine, 1974-1994" by Laura M. Carpenter in *The Journal of Sex Research*, May 1998. Read the article (with careful attention to the conclusions) and answer the following questions:

  a. According to the article, what sexual behaviors might be influenced by the way sexual scripts are portrayed in Seventeen Magazine?

  b. How might other teen magazines differ from Seventeen Magazine in the way that girls and women are portrayed?

  c. How do magazines geared toward adolescent boys portray male and female experiences of sexuality and romance?

10. *Sex in Other Cultures*

Examine the sexual norms and practices of another society or subculture. (Using InfoTrac, search words such as **Brazil and sex**, **Sweden and sex**, or **China and sex**). Compare and contrast these findings with you own culture in terms of one or more of the following topics:
- Sex Education
- Non-marital Sex
- Pre-marital Sex
- Sex in the media
- Sexual Double Standard
- The Role of Religion on Sexual Attitudes and Practices
- Sexual Diversity

11. *Viewing Sex Historically*

Do sexual attitudes and behaviors become more relaxed over time? Or do they fluctuate with the changing times, becoming more conservative or liberal as the wider culture does?

Using InfoTrac, search **history of sex**, and compare any decade of the twentieth century with the present. You might compare the present with the 1960s or the 1920s, both decades that saw major transformations in sexual attitudes and practices.

In your comparison between the present and a specific decade of the past, indicate which of the following factors played a role in determining sexual attitudes and behavior.

- War
- The Economy
- The Media
- Politics / Government Policies
- Health
- Religion
- Medical and Scientific Advances

Are there other circumstances that played a role in defining sex for that era?

12. *Sex in a Diverse United States*

Our sexual ideas and practices vary according to the cultural values and traditions of our communities. Choose a U.S. subculture, a specific ethnicity, race, or religious group that distinguishes itself from the mainstream or majority culture in one or more ways. Then use InfoTrac to find information about sexual practices that prevail in that group. If information is difficult to find, discuss why that might be. Based on the material you find, discuss the following:

    a.   How does the group's practices set them apart, if at all, from others?

    b.   Are the sexual ideas and practices of this group stigmatized by the media or the wider culture? If so, how and why?

Chapter 2

Sex Research: Methods and Problems

1.   *Why Study Sex?*

Researchers study sexual attitudes and practices in order to understand, predict, or influence sexual behavior.

Using InfoTrac, read one article listed for the search term **sexual attitudes.**

       a.   Determine whether the goal of the study is to understand, predict, or influence behavior.

       b.   Indicate how the research results might be implemented in policy.

2.   *Identifying the Research Method Used*

Using InfoTrac, look up the following 3 articles.

       "Relationship Functioning and Sexuality among People with Multiple Sclerosis" by M. P. McCabe, in *The Journal of Sex Research*, Fall 2002.

       "Ambiguous Stimuli: Sex is in the Eye of the Beholder" by C. O. Castille and J. H. Geer, in *Archives of Sexual Behavior*, April 1993.

       "Case Study: Sex Reassignment in a Teenage Girl" by W. G. Reiner, in *Journal of the American Academy of Child and Adolescent Psychiatry*, June 1996.

For each, determine the following:

       a.   What research method was used in the reported study? (experimental, survey, case study)

       b.   How were you able to make the above determination?

       c.   How could you study the same topic using a different research design?

3. *Understanding Research Methods*

The methods used in research are determined by the question you want to answer. Discover more about one of the following topics:

- **Condom Use**
- **Viagra**
- **Sex Reassignment Surgery / Sex Change Procedures**
- **Teen Sex Attitudes**

Using InfoTrac, find one article based on a research study that addresses your topic. Then describe the method used: case study, survey, direct observation, experimental method, other.

    a.   What research question was addressed in the research?

    b.   Does the method used seem appropriate for the question asked?

    c.   What are the advantages and disadvantages of using this method?

Think about what other method could have been used to explore the same topic?

    d.   State research question (What do you want to know?)

    e.   What are the advantages and limitations of this method?

4. *Experimental Sex Research: Dependent and Independent Variables*

To better understand how researchers study cause and effect, consider specific research examples that use dependent and independent variables.

Using InfoTrac, find five articles that report results from sex research. For each one:

    a.   Determine which method or methods researchers used (case study, survey, direct observation, and experimental method).

    b.   Identify one article that utilizes an experimental method, and for that study indicate the dependent and independent variables.

    c.   How does the researcher describe the relationship between these variables (dependent and independent), and how do the variables relate to statements of cause and effect?

5.   *Scientific Sex Research: Understanding the Journal Article*

Researchers use a common format when writing about their own studies. Familiarizing yourself with this format will help you better extract important information from the articles you read. Research articles are usually divided into 6 sections (Abstract, Introduction, Method, Results, Discussion, and References) and each section contains specific types of information.

Use InfoTrac to locate the following article on **safe sex behavior** entitled "Australian and South African Undergraduates' HIV-Related Knowledge, Attitudes, and Behaviors" by Anthony Smith, Richard de Visser, Adebowale Akande, Doreen Rosenthal, and Susan Moore, in *Archives of Sexual Behavior*, June 1998. Read the entire article and note what types of information the authors include in each of the following sections:

- Abstract
- Introduction
- Method
- Results
- Discussion
- References

The research format described above is used for primary research articles -- articles that describe a specific study (or series of studies) conducted by the authors themselves. Other articles may be written to review other people's research or to discuss past research in a theoretical context (these are often referred to as secondary sources). Search the InfoTrac database using **sexuality research** as a key word and find at least one additional primary research article that reports research in this format.

6.   *Critiquing a Journal Article: Detecting Bias in Research*

Choose an article from a standard research journal such as *Journal for Sexuality Research* that you believe includes some instance of bias (demographic bias, self-selection, non-response). Using the following questions, think critically about the research in order to evaluate the research presented.

a.   Does the title and/or abstract convey the limitations of the study?

b.   What are the potential sources of bias in this research?

c.   Do you have enough information to determine whether the research is biased?

d.   What additional information do you think should have been included in the article?

e.   Given instances of bias, suggest possible corrections.

f. How does the knowledge of the bias affect your overall understanding of the topic under consideration?

g Overall, do you believe the findings of this research? Overall, do you think it is good research?

7. *Operational Definitions: How is Behavior Measured in Sexuality Research?*

Operational definitions refer to the way in which a concept is measured or defined in research. Search articles on InfoTrac using the key term **sexual arousal.** Compare your answers to the following questions for each of the articles.

a. How was sexual arousal defined and measured?

b. What factors might have led the researchers to define and measure sexual arousal in the way that they did.

c. If sexual arousal had been defined or measured differently, do you think the authors would still have the same results?

8. *Obstacles of Sex Research*

All research projects can encounter difficulties in obtaining funding, non-response, volunteer bias, and so on. Special problems are bound to arise when the research is about sex: funders may back away, interviewees may decline to answer certain questions, participants may not be truthful in reporting their sexual experiences and attitudes, etc.

Using InfoTrac, find information about the **Kinsey Report, Masters and Johnson**, the **National Health and Social Life Survey,** or other studies.

a. What difficulties did the researchers encounter in finding funding for their work?

b. What sort of difficulties did the researchers encounter in obtaining reliable responses from the people they interviewed or observed?

c. What have critics said about the report? What do they see as its main limitations? What are its main strengths?

9. *Evaluating Sex Research*

Can you believe everything you read? How reliable are the sex surveys that appear in popular magazines?

Using InfoTrac, find one article that reports results from a random-sample or other academically rigorous research study. Find a second one that reports findings from an unscientific magazine survey.

Compare their methods by answering the following questions:

a. What are the researchers' credentials? What are their potential biases? Are they affiliated with or funded by any group (such as a pharmaceutical company or advertised product) that might be interested in a particular finding or result?

b. Was the method appropriate to the question being posed?

c. Was the sample sufficiently large and appropriately administered to avoid bias?

d. Are surveys that use non-representative samples (such as the popular magazine surveys) simply misleading or do they have any value? If so, what?

10. *Considering the Sample in Sexuality Research*

Using InfoTrac, locate three research articles on the same aspect of sexuality (i.e., **safe sex behavior, abstinence, orgasm**, etc.). Read the articles and answer the following questions:

a. Describe participant characteristics (age, race, sexual orientation, education, social economic status, etc.).

b. How many individuals participated in this research? How did researchers locate and recruit participants?

c. In what ways do participants reflect the general population? How does this influence the way you interpret the results of this research?

d. In what ways are the participants unique from the general population? How does this influence the way you interpret the results of this research?

11. *What Social Factors Influence Sexual Behavior?*

Sexual behavior varies individually, but research can also reveal patterns that vary according to social factors or institutions such as religion, age, gender, ethnicity, nationality, sexual orientation, and other factors.

Using InfoTrac, find, read, and discuss "Sociocultural Correlates of Permissive Sexual Attitudes: A Test of Reiss's Hypothesis about Sweden and the United States" by Martin S. Weinberg, Ilsa Lottes, and Frances M. Shaver in *The Journal of Sex Research*, February 2000.

        a,   What social factors do the authors compare?

        b.   What kinds of data did the authors use? Are the results convincing? What are the study's weaknesses?

        c.   Do their results change any assumptions you held about either the U.S. or Sweden?

12. *AIDS Research*

The effort to find a vaccine and cure for AIDS and to prevent the spread of HIV has been the focus of much sex research. Consider some of the characteristics of this important research.

Using InfoTrac, examine articles on AIDS research.

        a.   Find one example of each research method and indicate the question investigated:

- Experimental Method
- Survey Method

        b.   AIDS research tends to target particular social groups -- gay men and intravenous drug users, in particular. It is well known that HIV infection can occur through risky sexual behaviors independently of a person's social characteristics. Find one example of another social group that does not fit the traditional at-risk profile but whose sexual practices may make them susceptible to HIV infection.

        c.   Name one recent finding that indicates a social group that is increasingly at high risk of contracting HIV.

        d.   Name one recent finding that indicates a change in behaviors that may increase the incidence of the disease.

13.   *The Kinsey Reports*

Several recent articles have re-examined the work of **Alfred Kinsey** and questioned his research methods, motivations, or findings.

Using InfoTrac, read one or more of these critiques, and then discuss the following question:

Do you think the personal views or experiences of a researcher can influence his or her research? If so, is it to the benefit or detriment of the research? Explain your answer.

Chapter 3

Gender Issues

1.   *The Meanings of Sex and Gender*

The terms sex and gender are sometimes used interchangeably. However, the two words have specific definitions. Using InfoTrac, search articles using the keyword **sex**. Then search articles using the keyword **gender**. After browsing several articles for each, answer the following questions:

      a.   How are sex and gender defined by different authors?

      b.   Review the textbook definitions of the two terms. Are the articles using the terms in a way that is consistent with the textbook definition?

      c.   For each set of articles, what types of questions and/or issues are being addressed?

2.   *Cultural Notions of Masculinity and Femininity*

Cultural stereotypes of men and women shape our notions of **masculinity** and **femininity**. Using InfoTrac, search articles related to these two terms. Peruse the articles and then answer the following questions:

      a.   For your search under masculinity: What types of behaviors, emotions, and ways of thinking were discussed? Were these only discussed in terms of men?

      b.   For your search under femininity: What types of behaviors, emotions, and ways of thinking were discussed? Were these only discussed in terms of women?

      c.   How were men and women portrayed similarly and differently? Did the articles spend more time discussing similarities or differences? How do you think this affects the way men and women are perceived as "opposites?"

3. *Gender Roles: Cultural Variations*

"Sugar and spice and everything nice – that's what girls are made of."

"Boys will be boys."

These traditional characterizations of girls and boys are still heard in our society. They are not, however, cultural universals. Expectations about gender-appropriate behavior vary from one culture to another and differ among subcultures within the same society.

Using InfoTrac, search the phrase **gender roles** to find one example of a culture different from our own. Then describe for that society:

- The desired / expected qualities of girls / women

- The desired / expected qualities of boys / men

Then discuss the following:

a. What does this contrast suggest about the role of culture in defining gender roles?

b. What does this contrast suggest about the role of biology on gender? Are there gender universals that affect every culture? If so, what are they?

4. *Gender Socialization*

Boys and girls grow up facing social pressures to behave in gender-appropriate ways. An individual who deviates from those gender expectations may be criticized, ridiculed, or even punished.

First, write down two examples from your own experience of situations you observed or experienced in which a person failed to conform to gender expectations.

Then, using InfoTrac, search **gender role** or **gender socialization** to find at least two research articles about how gender-specific behavior is imposed on children.

Using your own experience and your research examples, write a brief response to the following:

a. In your view, why is gender conformity so strictly enforced?

b. Who is most likely to impose gender conformity on children (e.g., peers, family, teachers)?

c.   What is the influence of the media in encouraging children to self-impose gender-specific behaviors?

d.   Is one sex more likely than the other to be penalized for failing to conform to gender stereotypes? If so, why?

e.   Do you think boys and girls in our society have recently gained more leeway in deciding to adopt a variety of masculine and feminine behaviors? Give examples.

5. *Gender Revolution or Gender Evolution?*

Using InfoTrac, search articles on **gender roles**. Find one article that assesses changes in gender relations.

a.   Summarize the article's findings in writing. (Be sure to give the author, article title, journal title, volume number, pages, and date of the article you discuss).

b.   Compare information from the article with the experiences of men and women in your family's history regarding gender roles.

Outline first the shifts in social role and behavior of <u>women</u> in your family over the past three generations.

	EDUCATION	WORK	FAMILY ROLE	INTERESTS
Generation 1				
Generation 2				
Generation 3 (your own)				

Now do the same for <u>men</u> in your family.

	EDUCATION	WORK	FAMILY ROLE	INTERESTS
Generation 1				
Generation 2				
Generation 3 (your own)				

Study both charts and answer the following questions:

1. How much have gender roles changed between generations 1, 2, and 3?

2. In what areas have the distinctions between men and women changed the most? In what category have they changed the least?

3. How does your family's experience of gender role change compare to the findings of the article you summarized above?

6. *Physical Sex Differences*

Pick one of the following criteria currently thought to define a person's physical sex:

Chromosomal sex
Gonadal sex
Hormonal sex
Internal Reproductive Structures
External Genitalia
Sex Differences in the Brain

Using InfoTrac, find two articles on the topic you chose and use them to discuss the following:

a. Is this aspect of sexual difference solely biological or are there ways that cultural factors intervene? (For example, through medical intervention, socialization factors, or the fact that the brain forms *after* birth and in a social context, etc.)

b. Are there some ways in which this feature is similar in women and men? In your view, are the gender similarities or the gender differences more significant? Explain your answer.

c. For the factor you chose, assess the current level of scientific understanding. What issues remain unsettled? What questions remain to be researched?

7.   Beyond the Two Sexes?

Using InfoTrac, find the article entitled "The Five Sexes: Why Male and Female Are Not Enough" by Anne Fausto-Sterling, in *The Sciences*, March-April 1993.

Read the article and answer the following:

a.   Briefly, what is the basic idea supported by the author?

b.   What evidence does the author use to support her thesis?

c.   How does the existence of intersexed individuals challenge the current notions of biological sex, sex roles, masculinity, and femininity?

8.   Intersexuality

Consider the current debate about what treatment, if any, should be given to intersexed individuals. Some believe it is best to assign sex shortly after birth, performing genital surgery if necessary, so that every child fits a male or female standard model rather than remaining ambiguous. Others advocate the right of intersexuals to be free from having to choose one sex or the other and, especially, from having one chosen for them at birth by medical professionals or their own parents. Instead, they believe that society should change to accommodate more than two sexes.

Using InfoTrac and the Internet, find information on political advocacy and medical groups that represent each of these opposing views. Then compare the two perspectives.

For each source:

a.   Describe what evidence (medical cases, mental and physical health issues, socialization concerns) is used to argue each position. Note what is the disciplinary approach of the author or organization sponsoring the site.

b.   In your opinion, which side more adequately addresses the concerns of intersexuals today? Explain your choice.

9.   Transsexuality

A transsexual is a person whose gender identity (subjective sense of being male or female) does not fit his or her apparent biological sex. Some transsexuals undergo sex re-assignment procedures to bring their body into alignment with their gender identity.

This exercise will help you appreciate what a person experiences – physically, socially, and psychologically – when undergoing a sex change.

Using InfoTrac, search for a case study that describes the experiences of a **transsexual** (Either MTF or FTM) who undergoes sex change procedures.

   a.   Describe in order the steps the person undergoes to change sex. Include both psychological processes as well as any physical procedures.

   b.   List the social adjustments the person makes to re-enter society as a different sex. Be sure to address the following: Did the person's family, friends, and colleagues accept and support the change? How do people on the street react? What changes occurred in the person's sexual relationships, if any?

10.   Gender and Sexuality

Men and women are thought to experience sex differently. In our society, men are expected to want sex and to be more sexually assertive. Women are typically considered to be more interested in love than sex and to be less sexually active.

Using InfoTrac, find articles that deal with the sexual concerns or complaints that men and women bring to medical professionals. Then:

   a.   List the qualities and concerns of women and of men.

   b.   Discover whether these differences are primarily biological in origin or a result of socialization. Back up your opinion with evidence from the text and articles.

   c.   Give your prognosis for the future. Will women and men become more alike in terms of their sexual activity? Are there good reasons to retain differences in sexual behaviors and interests? What are they?

11. Applying the Definitions

The following concepts are distinct from one another. First, using your textbook write the definition of each:

- Sex Role
- Gender Identity
- Sexual Orientation

Second, using InfoTrac, look up articles using key terms **sex role, gender identity, sexual orientation**, and combinations of the three. Then answer the following:

a.   In what ways have the three concepts been researched individually?

b.   In what ways have the three concepts been researched together?

c.   Provide an example to describe how these three concepts are distinct.

d.   How would you describe your sex role, gender identity, and sexual orientation? How does one influence the other in your own self-identification?

Chapter 4

Female Sexual Anatomy and Physiology

1. *Women and Genital Anatomy*

Although anatomy would seem to be a straightforward matter of describing what can be observed in the body, anatomy – including genital anatomy – is a dynamic field. Today experts debate about what labels to apply and how to understand the function of sexual organs in women.

Using InfoTrac, look up these terms: **clitoris, G-spot, vagina, female ejaculation, female genitals**.

Choose one aspect of female genital anatomy or physiology.

Then consider the following:

     a.   What controversies surround your topic?

     b.   Is your subject more often defined in terms of health or illness?

     c.   Is your topic a factor in female sexual pleasure? Is pleasure addressed in the articles you found?

     d.   Did you learn anything you did not know about this aspect of female genital anatomy?

     e.   What research questions remain for anatomists to address about your topic?

2. *Promoting Self-Exams*

Using InfoTrac, search articles using the key term **genital self-exam** and locate an article entitled "Ads Promote Genital Self-Exam" by Mitchel Zoler in *Medical World News*, August 1989. Read the article and answer the following:

     a.   What was the purpose for promoting genital self-exams?

     b.   Who was targeted for the ad campaign?

     c.   Describe the nature of the ad campaign. Do you think it would be effective? Who would be most influenced by this campaign?

Using InfoTrac, search articles using the key term **breast self-exam**. Find and read articles related to promotion of breast self-exams for women. Then answer the following:

    a.   How are issues of genital and breast self-exams similar and different?

    b.   How do the differences factor into the structure of self-examination promotion (both genital and breast)?

    c.   How would you design a campaign for promoting self-examination in women?

3.   Female Genital Mutilation

Health professionals and many women's rights advocates would like to see an end to **female genital mutilation (FGM)**. There are some who believe that, because the practice is woven deeply into a culture's beliefs and practices, change can only be initiated where the practice occurs by local women, not by outsiders.

Using InfoTrac, find research on **female genital mutilation (FGM)**.

    a.   Consider FMG from the perspective of the people who practice it. Using the example of a single cultural setting, describe the specific reasons why women practice FGM. (What do women themselves say about it? Why do they say they do it?)

    b.   List three potentially negative health effects of the practice.

    c.   Do you think international health officials should leave the eradication effort to local people or intervene energetically to put an end to FGM? Explain your answer.

4.   Consider the Source: Women's Sexual Health

Research indicates that women's magazines are the number one source for obtaining health information for women. Using InfoTrac, search **women's sexual health** two times. The first time, check the "only referred publications" option. The second time, search all sources. Then answer the following questions:

    a.   How are women's sexual health issues presented in academic and mainstream publications?

    b.   Across the two forums: Were the same topics addressed? How was the information presented similarly and differently for the two audiences?

5. Representing Female Sexuality

Judy Chicago's *The Dinner Party* (see text) and **Eve Ensler's** play *The Vagina Monologues* are two examples of artistic work that has sought to put women's sexual anatomy on the table for open discussion.

Using InfoTrac, find out more about these or other works of art that deal with women's sexual health (search artists' names, work titles). Then discuss the following:

    a.   How were these works of arts received by the public? If there were criticisms, what were they?

    b.   Try the reversibility test: Imagine similar works of art that dealt with male genitals. Would such works have a different impact and meaning? What would these be?

    c.   Is there evidence that works like those of Chicago and Ensler have increased and improved public discussion of women's sexual anatomy and health?

    d.   Would you feel comfortable viewing these visual or verbal art works? Would you feel comfortable if you saw them in the company of men, of family members, and partners? Explain why you feel as you do.

    Bonus: Name and describe another art performance work that deals with female sexuality.

6. Menstruation

Recent research on menstruation suggests that the environment (both social and physical) has an effect on women's menstrual cycles.

Using InfoTrac, consider two or more recent articles about menstruation. Then:

    a.   List the specific social, physical, or environmental factors that are thought to influence menstrual patterns such as age of **menarche, PMS, menstrual synchrony**, etc.

    b.   Do you think there is convincing evidence that environmental factors affect menstrual patterns? Explain your answer.

7. *Information for Girls about Menarche*

Do you remember when you first learned about menstruation? Describe. (Your answer is likely to be different depending on whether you are male or female.) Include answers to these questions: Did you receive information at school? From your parents? Did you see or hear about it in movies, TV shows, or ads? Which ones? Were your impressions largely positive or negative?

Choose one of the following activities:

a. Ask one woman and one man of your parents' generation when and how they heard about menstruation. How did people in their generation talk about the phenomenon? Where did they get their information?

b. Using InfoTrac, find out what researchers know about the effects of timely education about menarche. Why do you think this might be important?

8. *Medical Interventions*

Using InfoTrac, consider articles on one of the following two medical interventions:

Pap Smear
Hysterectomy

Review the articles on your chosen topic. Then:

a. Summarize the trends in research

b. Consider the socioeconomic factors that influence the implementation of these procedures, such as cost, insured versus uninsured populations, racial category, and nationality.

9. *Breast Health*

Using InfoTrac, review recent research on ways to prevent, treat, and cure **breast cancer**.

Use the InfoTrac resources to:

a. Suggest two ways in which women themselves can reduce their chances of contracting the disease.

b. Name two treatments that show promise for treating the disease.

10. *Menopause and Women's Health in the Second Half of Life*

Using InfoTrac, read articles on **hormone replacement therapy** (HRT).

Make a chart showing the pros and cons of taking supplemental hormones after menopause. List health factors that may be affected by HRT (example: high blood pressure, heart disease, osteoporosis, breast cancer). Then for each one, discuss whether the available articles suggest HRT improves or may threaten that aspect of health.

Then discuss the following:

a. Do you think there is convincing evidence about the safety, benefits, and harms of HRT? What questions remain?

b. What do you think of the advertising campaigns for HRT by drug companies (often using glamorous and well-known women)? Do you think the ads improve or diminish women's ability to make informed decisions about HRT?

11. *Sexuality: Are Women and Men Really That Different?*

Using InfoTrac, find the article "Truth and Consequences: Using the Bogus Pipeline to Examine Sex Differences in Self-Reported Sexuality" by M. G. Alexander & T. D. Fisher, in *The Journal of Sex Research*, February 2003. Read the article and then answer the following:

a. What research question was asked? What research method did the authors use?

b. What was the major finding of this research report? How is this consistent with the psychosocial understanding of sexuality?

c. If you were asked about your sexual behaviors or attitudes, do you think you would be influenced by normative expectations? How do these normative expectations differ for men and women?

Chapter 5

Male Sexual Anatomy and Physiology

1. *The Penis*

Men tend to think of their penis as a single entity, but it actually has many different parts and several functions.

To better understand what lies beneath the skin, answer the following questions. Consult your textbook, or use the following InfoTrac terms: **penis, urethra, spongy body (*corpora spongiosum*), cavernous bodies (*corpora cavernosa*), glans, male genitals.**

      a.   What kind of tissue surrounds the urethra? What tissue makes up the glans?

      b.   How does an erection occur? Which parts of the penis change to make it erect?

2. *Cultural Notions of the Penis*

A common concern of men in our society is penis size, even though size rarely affects function and is not the determinant of a female partner's pleasure in sex.

Why do you think the belief that "bigger is better" is so prevalent in our culture?

Using InfoTrac, explore this and other cultural ideas about the penis, either in our own or other societies. Choose one topic, using search terms such as:

      Kama Sutra
      Priapus
      Phallus
      Male Sexuality and (name of culture or country)

Briefly describe the belief, its origin or basis, and how it influences sexual behavior and health.

3.   *Circumcision*

A majority of men in the United States are circumcised shortly after birth. What do you think of this widespread medical procedure?

Using InfoTrac, look up **circumcision** and explore the ongoing controversy about the procedure. Based on your readings, describe:

a.   The reasons (religious, traditional, medical) boys may be expected to undergo circumcision.

b.   The percentage of U.S. newborn boys who have the procedure. Note whether that number is going up or down.

c.   The reasons critics oppose the procedure.

d.   Recent evidence that being circumcised may help prevent the spread of STDs among adults.

e.   What do you think? Use your review of the evidence about circumcision to support your view.

4.   *Semen*

Using InfoTrac, examine one example of current research about health issues involving one of the following, all body parts that play a role in semen production:

seminiferous tubules
epididymis
vas deferens
seminal vesicles
prostate gland
Cowper's gland

Briefly describe the health issue being addressed, the nature of the research, and its conclusions.

5.   *Erection, Ejaculation, and Orgasm*

Using InfoTrac, explore these three aspects of sexual function: **erection, ejaculation, and orgasm.** For each:

a.   Define the term (using your text).

b.   Consider how they are related. Does ejaculation always occur with orgasm, or are they separate? Does erection always lead to ejaculation? If not, what are the effects on a man?

c.   What are some of the main health concerns regarding sexual response in men, according to your exploration of the articles in InfoTrac.

BONUS: Do any or all of these also occur in women? (On InfoTrac, look up **female ejaculation, sexual response,** and **orgasm**).

6.   *Sex Differences in Adolescence: A Look at First Ejaculation*

Using InfoTrac, search words **first ejaculation** or **semenarche**, find the article entitled "I've Never Thought About It: Contradictions and Taboos Surrounding American Males' Experiences of First Ejaculation (Semenarche)" by L. Frankel in *The Journal of Men's Studies*, Fall 2002.

Read the article and answer the following:

a.   Why do you think there has been little research on first ejaculation?

b.   How do experiences of first ejaculation differ across cultures? Provide some examples.

c.   Do you think semenarche and menarche are experienced similarly? According to this article, how are male and female adolescent experiences different? How is this related to **gender roles, sexual stereotypes, and the sexual double standard**?

7.   *Genital Health Issues*

Using InfoTrac, explore some current concerns about one of the following:

testicular cancer
penile cancer

Then answer the following questions:

a.   What populations (age, ethnicity, other characteristics) are most susceptible to this disease?

b.   What can men do to self-screen for the disease? What signs or symptoms should men look for?

8.   *Focus on Men's Sexual Health*

Find the following article on InfoTrac: "Missing Men: Addressing Sexual Health Care Needs" from *Contraceptive Technology Update*, June 2002. Read the article and answer the following questions:

a.   What issues are raised in the article?

b.   What are the obstacles to men's sexual health care?

c.   What psychosocial issues are raised in the article? How does an understanding of gender roles explain the way in which men use the health care system for sexual health issues?

9.   *Consider the Source: Men's Sexual Health*

Using InfoTrac, search **men's sexual health** two times. The first time, check the "only referred publications" option. The second time, search all sources. Then answer the following questions:

a.   How are men's sexual health issues presented in academic and mainstream publications?

b.   Across the two forums: Were the same topics addressed? How was the information presented similarly and differently for the two audiences?

10. *Prostate Cancer*

Prostate cancer is the second leading cause of cancer death for U.S. men after lung cancer.

Using InfoTrac, search **prostate cancer** and explore the following:

a. Is the rate of prostate cancer in the U.S. rising, falling, or remaining steady? What population characteristics, social habits or medical advances are affecting this trend?

b. Regaining sexual function after prostate cancer treatment has been aided by **Viagra** (sildenafil citrate). Explain why this drug helps some men affected by this disease.

11. *Viagra versus Birth Control: A Debate*

Using InfoTrac, find the article "Gender Discrimination within the Reproductive Health Care System: Viagra v. Birth Control" by L. A. Hayden, in *Journal of Law and Health*, Summer 1998.

a. Describe the issue raised in the article. Why is this issue important?

b. How do the following issues play into the debate? **health insurance, gender roles, sexual double standard, socioeconomic status**

c. Using InfoTrac, read about other issues of gender and sexual health. How are those issues similar to or different from the Viagra / birth control issue?

Chapter 6

Sexual Arousal and Response

1.   *Hormones and Desire*

Recent research indicates that the hormone testosterone is linked to sexual desire in both men and women.

Search articles on **testosterone** and explore the following issues:

a.   What evidence or studies show that testosterone affects desire?

b.   What evidence is there that **testosterone-replacement therapy** (TRT) improves sexual desire and function?

c.   What undesirable side-effects can TRT have in women? In men?

2.   *The Brain and Sex*

It is often said that the biggest and most important sexual organ is the brain. We could not experience the physical pleasure of sex without it. The cerebral cortex is considered to be where language, conscious thinking, and fantasies, including sexual fantasies, occur. The limbic system, in contrast, is thought to be the part of the brain that responds to physical and chemical stimuli such as touch and smell.

Using InfoTrac, review recent articles on these two parts of the brain and their role in sexual response. Then discuss the following:

a.   Is either system dominant in its influence on feelings of desire and sexual excitement?

b.   Are there gender distinctions in the way the brains works in sex?

c.   What does the research say about the link between the brain, sex, and love?

3.   Gender, the Senses, and Sexual Desire

Women are thought to link sexual desires with emotion and romance, while men respond to visual stimuli. What evidence do we have of this? Explore InfoTrac sources to address the following:

a.   How would you explain research that found that women respond physically to visual erotica but are less willing to acknowledge that they do?

b.   Is there evidence from other cultures that any gender difference may not be hardwired but might be culturally instilled?

4.   Cultural Variations in Sexual Arousal

The human brain grows a great deal after birth, when a person is learning language and living in a cultural context. What we learn to consider sexually desirable and arousing depends upon how our brain is conditioned as we grow up in a particular social setting. Our sexual socialization also varies by gender, sexual orientation, and other social and individual factors.

Using InfoTrac, explore how the body areas our culture considers sexy might <u>not</u> be seen as erotic in another society.

a.   Is there cross-cultural variation in what body parts are considered sexually arousing? Give two examples.

b.   **Erogenous zones** may also vary by culture. Are the same parts of the body people find aroused by touch the same ones that are considered sexy to look at? Use our own society as your example.

5.   Conceptualizing Sexual Response: Recent Research

Using InfoTrac, find the "Sexual Modes Questionnaire: Measure to Access the Interaction among Cognitions, Emotions, and Sexual Response" by P. J Nobre and J. Pinto-Gouveia in *The Journal of Sex Research*, November 2003.

Read the article and answer the following:

a.   Why did the researchers believe there was need to develop a new measure on sexual response (the Sexual Modes Questionnaire – SMQ)?

b.   What does this new measure add to our understanding of sexuality?

c. How did the male and female versions of the SMQ differ? How were they similar? Why was it necessary to have two different versions?

d. How does the wording of the scale apply to individuals with same- or other-sex partners?

6. *Aphrodisiacs and Sexual Stimulants*

An **aphrodisiac** is a substance thought to increase sexual desire or capacity.

Explore examples of aphrodisiacs or **sexual stimulants** on InfoTrac, then answer the following:

a. Is there an aphrodisiac used commonly in your community or among your friends or family? If so, what is it?

b. What is the most commonly used aphrodisiac in the United States?

c. Look up one commonly used aphrodisiac in another society (China, Brazil, Turkey)

d. Name two foods thought to be sexual stimulants.

For each of these, consider whether there is evidence that the product is safe and has a positive effect on the quality of sex.

7. *From Arousal to Orgasm: His and Hers*

Masters and Johnson described the sexual response pattern as occurring across four stages: excitement, plateau, orgasm, and resolution. Yet their description is just a guideline; most sex researchers agree that the subjective experience of sex varies.

Consider how, in general, the sexual response of women and men is both similar and different.

a. What is the best way to know if a woman is aroused? What indicates a man is sexually excited?

b. How do you know if a man has reached orgasm? How do you know when a woman has had an orgasm?

c. Do you think physiologists have fully explained arousal and orgasm? Do you think most adults are well informed about how sexual response occurs? Why or why not?

8.   *Multiple Orgasms*

Both men and women have been known to have **multiple orgasms**. For some, this phenomenon just happens, while others practice in order to have more than one orgasm in a single sexual encounter.

Search InfoTrac and use your book to discuss the following:

a.   What are the physical, psychological, or social impediments that might prevent men from experiencing multiple orgasms? What are those for women?

b.   Do you think that multiple orgasms are easier physically for one sex (male or female)?

c.   What are some methods people have used to learn how to have multiple orgasms?

9.   *Researching Sexual Arousal and Response*

Using InfoTrac, search for articles using key terms **sexual arousal** or **sexual response**. Then answer the following:

a.   How is sexual arousal or sexual response defined and measured in each of the different articles?

b.   Would the research results have changed if the definition and/or measurement had been defined differently?

c.   Describe the participants used in the study. How might they be similar or different from the general population?

10.   *Defining Sex: Thinking about Language*

Sometimes the language used to describe sexual acts in research settings and in everyday life emphasize some experiences as more important than others. Think about the following examples:

- Using "sex" to refer to only intercourse
- Foreplay
- Oral sex

    a.   How do these and other terms affect the way we view the importance of different sexual behaviors?

    b.   How might they affect the way we view sexual activity in both a heterosexual and non-heterosexual context?

Using InfoTrac, search articles using key term **sexual behaviors.** Then:

    c.   Identify other words that may limit the way we define sexual behaviors.

    d.   Think of new wordings that may reflect a more inclusive understanding of sexual behaviors. Under what circumstances would you consider using this new terminology?

Chapter 7

Love, Attraction, Attachment, and Intimate Relationships

1. *What's Love Got to Do with It?*

Sexual love involves passion, commitment or attachment, and intimacy. Although love can be difficult to define and measure, researchers have found that feeling connected to and cared for by others has profound health and social consequences.

Using InfoTrac, list and briefly describe some of the ways the absence, presence, or quality of **love** affects human health. Then:

    a.   Discuss whether the various kinds of love (romantic, companionate, passionate) have particular positive health effects. If yes, what are they?

    b.   Discuss whether the various kinds of love (romantic, companionate, passionate) have particular negative health effects. If yes, what are they?

2. *Defining Love*

Using InfoTrac, locate the following article entitled "Passionate Love and Anxiety: A Cross-Generational Study" by Al. Y. Wang, and H. T. Nguyen in *The Journal of Social Psychology*, August 1995.

Read the article with special attention to the Passionate Love Scale used. Then answer the following:

    a.   How is love being measured? What types of questions are used in the Passionate Love Scale?

    b.   What questions from the Passionate Love Scale might you also include on a scale of Companionate Love? What additional questions might you use?

    c.   Do you think love is defined differently across different groups of people (across generation, culture, etc.)?

3.   *Love and Romance*

Using InfoTrac, find the article entitled "Romantic Behaviors of University Students: A Cross-Cultural and Gender Analysis in Puerto Rico and the United States" by J. A. Quiles in *College Student Journal*, September 2003. Read the article and answer the following:

   a.   What is the purpose of this research study?

   b.   What were participants asked to do? How were the data collected?

   c.   Study the behaviors listed in Table 1. How would you have ranked the behaviors? What group included in the study was your response most like?

   d.   How did definitions of romance differ across population (Puerto Rico and U.S.) and gender (female and male)?

   e.   This research was conducted only with university students. Had the sample included non-students, do you think the results would have been different? Why or why not?

4.   *Theories of Love*

Use InfoTrac to explore **sociobiological** approaches to love, sexual relationships, and commitment. See also theories based on a similar perspective known as **evolutionary psychology** and articles on **reproductive success**.

   a.   First, outline the position of the evolutionary psychologists, giving their explanations for how and why people fall in love. How does love and attraction differ, according to this view, for women and men?

   b.   Does research about women's and men's actual preferences support this theory?

   c.   What are other possible explanations for such trends as women's preference for older, richer men and men's preference for younger, good-looking women? What alternative explanations do critics of evolutionary psychology give?

5.   *Types of Love*

Using InfoTrac, search key terms **romantic love, companionate love, consummate love, liking, empty love, fatuous love, infatuation,** and **empty love**.

   a.   Given your search results, are different types of love equally researched and considered in the literature? What does this say about the way in which love is conceptualized in both the academic and popular realm?

   b.   Does research using non-heterosexual populations emphasize the same types of love? What does this say about the way in which we conceptualize the love relationships in heterosexual and non-heterosexual individuals?

6.   *Why We Do the Things We Do: Attraction, Dating, and Marriage*

Use InfoTrac to find the following two articles:

"Age Differences in Dating and Marriage: Reproductive Strategies or Social Preferences?" by A. Davis in *Current Anthropology*, June 1998.

"Physical Attractiveness and the "Nice Guy Paradox": Do Nice Guys Really Finish Last?" by G. C. Urbaniak and P. R. Kilmann in *Sex Roles: A Journal of Research*, November 2003.

Read the articles and then answer the following:

   a.   What theoretical perspectives do each of the articles take in understanding attraction, dating, and marriage?

   b.   Describe how you think the research would be designed differently if it had originated from a different theoretical perspective.

   c.   What do you think? What do you think is the single most important factor in determining dating and marriage behaviors?

7. *Styles of Loving*

Find the following articles using InfoTrac.

"Sexual Aggression and Love Styles: An Exploratory Study" by D. B. Sarwer, S. C. Kalichman, J. R. Johnson, J. Early, and S. A. Ali, in *Archives of Sexual Behavior*, June 1993.

"Love Styles among Portuguese Students" by F. Neto, in *The Journal of Psychology*, September 1994.

Both of these articles utilize Lee's theory of love differently. Read these articles and:

    a.   Briefly describe Lee's theory. Does each research article understand Lee's theory in a similar way? Why or why not?

    b.   How is Lee's theory being used in each study?

    c.   How does each research finding change the way you view Lee's theory?

    d.   How does each research finding change the way you view love?

8. *Love in the Media*

Television, music, and film may be the forms of media that most influence our ideas of love. Using InfoTrac, examine articles on **love and media** and **romance**.

Then answer the following:

    a.   What evidence is there that the media influences the way we experience falling in love?

    b.   In the medium that you view or hear most frequently, do stories include mostly companionate or passionate love, or some combination of the two? Give an example from the medium of your choice.

9. Individualistic versus Family-Based Marriage

Some societies expect individuals to marry according to the wishes of the family or community. In others, such as the United States, people believe that each individual freely chooses his or her spouse.

Using InfoTrac, find research on the experiences of people from societies with family-based marriage who live in the United States.

    a.   What difficulties do they encounter when looking for a spouse while living in the United States?

    b.   What factors influence whether or not they follow the model from their society of origin (or of their parents) or of the society where they now live?

    c.   What do you think? In a society like the United States, where the ideal is romantic love based on an individual's desire, does the family still play a role in the choice of marital partner? What is that role? Give examples.

10. The Chemistry of Love

Scientists have discovered much about the chemical processes that occur when we are passionately in love.

Using InfoTrac, look up one of the following: **phenylethylamine (PEA), norepinephrine, dopamine, or endorphins.**

Then discuss:

    a.   What is the effect on the body of this chemical?

    b.   In what other context does the body produce this chemical?

    c.   Is long-term exposure to the chemical good for health?

    d.   Is it possible for a person in a long-term, committed relationship to continue to enjoy its positive effects?

    e.   Is there evidence this chemical can cause "love addiction"?

11. *Who Do You Love?*

Your text suggests that we choose intimate partners in ways that suggest the importance of proximity, similarity, reciprocity, and physical attractiveness.

Pick one of these features and, using InfoTrac, review some of the related social or psychological research about mate selection. Then answer the questions for your topic:

a. **Proximity:** Find research that lists the situations and contexts where a person is most likely to meet a partner. Has this changed over time?

b. **Similarity:** Are we more or less likely today to become intimate with someone socio-economically similar to ourselves as Americans were 100 years ago? Why or why not?

c. **Reciprocity:** Do men and women show their love differently? Do women expect the same things from men to show their dedication that men expect from women?

d. **Physical Attractiveness:** Do heterosexual women and men give the same value to physical attractiveness? Does either sex have a more rigid or predefined model of what a mate should look like? Has this pattern changed over time? Are these standards the same or different for gay men and lesbians?

12. *Love and Sex*

Sexual activity enhances feelings of love. It can also occur independently of love. In our society, there are a wide variety of views about when and at what point in a relationship a couple has sex. Do partners, or potential partners, always agree?

Review the research on InfoTrac about what women and men look for in a relationship when deciding about having sex.

a. Have the perspectives of women and men become more alike over time? Or is there a significant difference based on gender?

b. Deciding to have sex can be especially important for a person who has never before engaged in partner sex. Do women and men face different issues when faced with their "first time"? What are they?

13. Healthy and Lasting Love

Many ingredients go into a good sexual partnership. Using InfoTrac, explore some of the characteristics of couples in **long-term relationships** or **marriages**. Examine factors that have to do with the couple as well as external factors (family, social disapproval, economic problems, etc.). Then discuss the following:

   a.   How important is sex in the context of all the issues a couple faces? Is it more important for one gender than another?

   b.   Are there special challenges that people face when they are in same-sex love relationships? Are there some advantages they enjoy that other-sex couples do not? Explain.

14. Jealousy and Relationships

Using InfoTrac, search key term **jealousy** and answer the following questions:

   a.   In what ways is jealousy being written about and researched? What types of research methods are used to study jealousy? In what types of relationships is jealousy being considered (heterosexual and non-heterosexual love relationships, friendships, marriages, etc.)

   b.   How is jealousy being measured in these studies? How does this affect the results obtained in the research?

Chapter 8

Communication in Sexual Behavior

1.   *Talking about Sex*

Experts agree that a good exchange of information is essential in a healthy sexual relationship (and in any single sexual encounter!). Communication may be the single most important way to make partner sex better, and it is essential for ensuring safer sex practices.

Talking about sex can be extremely difficult, however. Sometimes people engage in sexual behaviors they do not want because they are unable to talk to their partner. Alternatively, sometimes people do not engage in sexual behaviors that they might prefer because they do not voice their desires.

In your experience, what are the most common obstacles to talking about sex? Using InfoTrac, compare your experience with research on this issue using search terms such as **language and sex, sex and ethnicity, sexual shame, sex and communication, sexual taboo, sexual violence, sexual terminology, sexual exploration.**

Discuss three obstacles to sexual communication. In each case, suggest how the obstacle affects sexual relationships and give possible solutions.

2.   *Talking Across Sexual Topics*

> a.   How does your communication vary across different sexual topics? How is sexuality discussed in your different relationships (i.e., parents, partners, friends, etc.)?

> b.   Using InfoTrac, search key term **sex and communication** and consider the way sex is discussed across different topics and relationships. Think about the ways in which your experience is reflected in the literature.

3. *Gendered Communication Styles*

For most couples, including same-sex partners, gendered styles of communication can erect barriers to getting your ideas across. Linguist **Deborah Tannen** explored this problem in her book *You Just Don't Understand: Women and Men in Conversation*.

Using InfoTrac, explore Tannen's arguments and those of other researchers on **gender and language**, and **sex and language**. Then discuss the following:

    a.   What are some typical qualities of men's speech? Of women's?

    b.   What are some ways in which heterosexual couples can overcome those differences?

    c.   What role can media (Internet, TV, film, music, etc.) play in opening up conversations about sex?

    d.   In what way might power differences between men and women explain any gender differences in communication that exist?

4. *Applying Tannen's Gendered Communication Theory*

Using InfoTrac, find the article entitled "Conversations On-Line: Girls' Rapport Talk and Boys' Report Talk" by K. Michel, in *Women and Language*, Spring 1994. Read the article and answer the following:

    a.   What was the purpose of this study?

    b.   Who were the participants in the study?

    c.   What was the research setting / scenario used?

    d.   What findings were reported? And what did the author conclude about these findings?

    e.   What are some alternative explanations for why this research did not follow Tannen's predictions?

    f.   Do you think gender differences in communication styles differ across the life span, have changed with the times, or differ across situations?

5. *Culture and Styles of Communication*

Styles of communication also vary substantially by culture or subcultures, even when partners both speak the same language. Because of these differences, partners may have distinct expectations about sex.

Explore InfoTrac for **sexual surveys** or studies that involve a country other than the United States. (Large surveys have been conducted in Finland, France, United Kingdom and several other nations. There are also qualitative studies on other communities.)

Compare the United States and the other culture you chose.

a. Are people in that culture likely to talk to their partners openly about sex? Do they tend to be more or less open than in the United States?

b. What role does the media play in defining sex? How is sex portrayed there (openly, not at all, etc.)?

c. Is there sex education in the schools? Does it give a broad range of information? Is it based on religious or scientific principles?

d. What are the culture's expectations about gender and sex? Specifically, are women and men expected to enjoy sex equally? Do both genders share in sexual decision making and responsibility?

6. *Non-Verbal Communication*

One of the biggest impediments to people talking about sex is the belief that good sex just comes "naturally" and that a lover should magically know what his or her partner wants without having to ask. In this view, all sexual communication should be physical and non-verbal.

Using InfoTrac, explore the research on **sexual signals**.

a. When can non-verbal communication enhance the quality of sexual interaction?

b. When can it be dangerous?

c. Do you think there are instances where talking can destroy sex? If so, when and why?

7. *Making Decisions About Sexual Behavior*

When couples cannot or do not talk, they may not be in full agreement about engaging in sex or in certain sexual behaviors. The message that sex advice columns and sex experts give over and over to couples is to keep communication open and to ask questions.

Saying NO. Using InfoTrac, find a source that offers techniques for making sure that your desires are clearly understood by your partner, including your desire not to be sexual.

> a. Who is usually the audience for articles indicating how to "say NO"?

> b. Are there articles providing advise for ensuring that you do not violate your partner's wishes regarding sexual behavior? If so, who is usually the audience for such articles?

Making yourself understood is not only important the first time you have sex with a person, but also in ongoing relationships. You want to be sure that both you and your partner agree about trying a new type of sexual behavior, for example.

Sexual Scenario. Write a scene in which an established couple negotiates a new sexual activity. Use the techniques offered in your text and in the InfoTrac sources found above.

8. *Same-Sex Relationships and Communication*

Given gender differences in language styles, you might expect that same-sex couples would be able to communicate with greater ease. Talking about love and sex with a same-sex partner may have some unique challenges, however.

Using InfoTrac, review the research on same-sex relations and communication and discuss both the advantages and special difficulties same-sex partners may have over other-sex partners.

9.   The Effects of Drugs and Violence on Communication

Using InfoTrac, review the literature on **sex and communication**. Two factors that may make communication more difficult:

- The use of alcohol and other drugs
- The experience of violence, whether in the current relationship or in the past

Examine one article that deals with one of the exacerbating factors. Then discuss how either alcohol or violence interferes with an individual's or a couple's ability to talk in useful ways about love and sex.

BONUS: Discuss how alcohol and violence are often interrelated.

10.   Sex as Communication

In what ways is sex used to communicate your feelings on larger relationship issues. Use InfoTrac to explore how sex facilitates or inhibits communication in a relationship. Consider research on the following:

- Sex as a way to end conflict in a relationship
- Sex as a signal of intimacy
- Withdrawal of sex as a sign of dissatisfaction

Chapter 9

Sexual Behaviors

1.   *What is Sex?*

Until recently, "sex" usually meant heterosexual vaginal intercourse. Does that definition still hold? If so, for whom?

Consider the various ways people define sex. Is kissing sex? Or is sex only when the genitals are involved?

Using InfoTrac, look up any one sexual activity discussed in the chapter (for example, oral sex or masturbation). Read what researchers report about how people view this activity and answer the following:

        a.   Have attitudes about this activity varied over time and in different places? If so, how? Give examples.

        b.   Are there some sectors of the population that have a strong opinion in favor or against this sexual activity? Explain who and why.

        c.   Where does this activity stand in relation to other sexual activities? Find research that indicates how common and how accepted the activity is.

        d.   What do you think? Is the activity you choose "sex"?

2.   *Celibacy, Virginity, and Abstinence*

Search the key terms **celibacy, virginity,** and **abstinence**.

These words are sometimes used interchangeably, yet they have distinct meanings that indicate social values rather than actual sexual practice.

Briefly review several articles on each term and define all three in contrast to one another. Be sure to explain how abstinence is different from celibacy. Can a person be celibate without being a virgin? Can a person who is not a virgin become one? How?

3.   Sexual Activity and Sexual Education

Using InfoTrac, find 2-3 recent articles that present research findings about how sex education influences the sexual activity of young people.

Articles on this topic include:

"How Do Adults View Sex Ed?" in *Family Planning Perspectives*, September 1999.

"Liberals Itching to Take Abstinence: Only Courses to Court" in *Insight on the News*, January 2001.

"What to Tell the Children?" in *National Review*, September 2000.

Then, based on your review of the research, discuss the following:

a.   What are the pros and cons of abstinence-only education?

b.   Is there evidence that talking and teaching about sex encourages young people to become sexually active?

c.   At what age or grade does sex education most often begin? What topics does it include? Do most experts believe it is early enough and sufficiently complete? Why or why not?

d.   Is it best to isolate sex education from other parts of the curriculum or integrate it? Is it best to segregate boys and girls?

e.   Should sex education include information about sexual orientation?

BONUS: Describe the sex education curriculum in your secondary school. Was the information sufficient and timely? Why and why not?

4. *Masturbation*

Using InfoTrac, use the key term **masturbation** to research the following:

   a.   How have ideas about masturbation changed in the U.S. since the 19th century? Describe the common view of masturbation 150 years ago and how most people view it today. Have any attitudes about it remained the same?

   b.   According to researchers, do most people see masturbation as "real sex," that is, as a sexual activity in its own right, or as a substitute for sex with a partner?

Note how few citations there are for the search term **masturbation**. Although masturbation is the most commonly practiced form of sex, it is still taboo to advocate – or even discuss – this safest form of sex.

   c.   Report on the fallout after Clinton-era Surgeon General Dr. Jocelyn Elders asserted that masturbation should be taught in schools.

   d.   Based on your reading and your own experience, what are some of the reasons why masturbation is taboo.

5. *Oral Sex*

Some young people consider **oral sex (cunnilingus, fellatio)** to be a less serious, risky, or intrusive sort of sexual behavior than vagina intercourse. Some teens engage in it because it does not expose a woman to the risk of unwanted pregnancy.

Using InfoTrac, examine the trend among teens of postponing vaginal intercourse even though they are already engaging in oral sex.

   a.   What threat to health may be related to oral sex? How can those dangers be minimized?

   b.   How might the perception that oral sex is not "real sex" influence a person to agree to it even if he or she does not want to?

   c.   Are there benefits to young people engaging in oral sex (assuming they use safer-sex procedures)?

   d.   What role does the media play in the portrayal of oral sex among young people? About their view on oral sex in general?

6. Same-Sex Sexual Activity

Using InfoTrac, find and read the article entitled "Trends in Same-Gender Sexual Partnering, 1988-1998" by A. C. Butler in the *Journal of Sex Research*, November 2000.

   a.   List the social and legal changes that have occurred that, according to the researcher, suggest an increase in sex between people of the same gender.

Using several InfoTrac sources, discover survey and other research findings regarding the sexual activities same- and other-sex partners are most likely to engage in.

   a.   According to research, what is the most common sex act between two men? Two women? A man and a woman?

7. *Ethnic Differences in Sexual Decisions and Behaviors Among Women*

Using InfoTrac, find the article entitled "Ethnic Differences in Sexual Decisions and Sexual Behavior" by D. Quadagno, D. F. Sly, D. F. Harrison, I. W. Eberstein, and H. R. Soler in *Archives of Sexual Behavior*, February 1998. Read the article and answer the following questions:

   a.   What was the purpose of this research?

   b.   Describe participant characteristics. In what ways do the participants represent the diversity of the larger U.S. population?   In what ways are the participants unique?

   c.   What influenced the participants' decision making regarding sexual behavior? How did this vary across ethnic groups?

   d.   What influenced whether a woman engaged in vaginal, oral, and anal sex?

   e.   What questions regarding the topic remain unanswered?

   f.   Do you think that a similar study using men would have similar results? Why or why not?

8. *Sexual Fantasies*

Using InfoTrac, search the key term **sexual fantasies**. Find articles (both research articles and popular press articles) and consider the way in which sexual fantasies are discussed.

    a.   What topics related to sexual fantasies are most discussed in the literature?

    b.   Are sexual fantasies discussed differently for men and women?

    c.   In these articles, what is the assumed relationship between sexual fantasies and sexual behavior?

9. *Gender and Pleasure*

Using a variety of InfoTrac sources, determine which activities women and men say they find most pleasurable. (Your sources might include **sex surveys** or other primary research). Then, consider whether the following statements have basis in fact:

    a.   Women like romance and cuddling more than genital contact.

    b.   Men are only interested in genital sex and orgasm.

If gender differences do exist, to what do you attribute them? Anatomy? Sexual socialization? Discuss.

10. *Sex and Culture*

Compare information about **sexual activity** in different societies and subcultures. (You might choose the National Health and Social Life Survey for the United States and compare to similar surveys from Britain, France, or Finland. Or contrast United States ethnic and racial groups.)

For both cultures, consider the following:

    a.   Most common sexual activity

    b.   Greatest taboo

    c.   Status of sex-sex eroticism (Is it stigmatized? Outlawed? Accepted?)

    d.   Degree of sexual equity between women and men (consider, for example, rates of orgasm, issues of sexual initiation, etc.)

Chapter 10

Sexual Orientations

1.   *What is Sexual Orientation?*

Using InfoTrac, use the search term **sexual orientation** to locate 5-7 articles using the option to search for only referred publications. Use the articles to answer the following questions:

a.   How is sexual orientation defined in each of the articles? Do you feel like there is consistency in those definitions? Why or why not?

b.   Sexual orientation research may focus on an individual's **sexual orientation identity**, or it may rely on an individual's reported **attraction**, **behavior**, or **fantasies**. How are these aspects of sexuality similar or different? Are these aspects always aligned with one another? How do these aspects relate to identity?

2.   *Sexual Orientation*

What other terms are used to describe sexual orientation?   Using InfoTrac, explore articles related to sexual orientation. Consider the use of the following terms:

- **Sexual preference**
- **Affectional orientation**
- **Sexual minorities**
- **"Lifestyle" (versus life)**
- **Queer**
- **Non-heterosexually identified individuals**

a.   In what context are the above terms used? Are they used differently across academic and popular sources?

b.   How does the language being used change your understanding of the concept?

3. *What Determines Sexual Orientation?*

Is sexual orientation inscribed in the body? Recent research has explored possible hormonal, brain, and/or genetic factors as possible keys to sexual orientation. Other studies investigate how a person becomes oriented to same- or other-sex partners because of social experience, including early family interactions. Some theories employ a combination of biological and psychosocial explanations.

On InfoTrac, search **sexual orientation** and **cause** (as a key word), **gay gene, gay brain**, and examine one or more articles. Take special note of any work on heterosexuality. Then discuss the following:

   a.   What are the implications if sexual orientation were shown to be primarily biological? Which social groups would most welcome such a finding? Do you think such a finding is scientifically possible?

   b.   What are the implications of research showing that sexual orientation is primarily psychosocial?

4. *Can Sexual Orientation Be Changed?*

One of the reasons some people seek the "causes" of homosexuality is in order to encourage non-heterosexually identified individuals to become heterosexual. Using InfoTrac, look up **gay conversion, conversion therapy, or reparative therapy**.

   a.   What are the arguments used to support conversion therapy? Are there certain groups of individuals that are more likely to support conversion therapy?

   b.   What are the arguments used against conversion therapy? Are there certain groups of individuals that are more likely to argue against conversion therapy?

   c.   Regarding conversion therapy, what is the position of different medical and psychological associations?

   d.   What you think of attempts to "convert" lesbians and gay men to heterosexuality?

5.   *Explaining Sexual Orientation and Understanding Heterosexuality*

Using InfoTrac, use the search terms **sexual orientation** and **heterosexuality**. Survey the articles for the approach taken in understanding sexual orientation. Consider the following:

a.   Do articles spend equal time theorizing about what causes individuals to become heterosexual, homosexual, and bisexual? (i.e., Are there articles looking for the "heterosexual gene"?) And how does this impact the way we regard non-heterosexually identified individuals?

b.   How is heterosexuality defined and measured in research articles?

c.   Use InfoTrac to search for articles related to sexual orientation in both referred forums and in the popular press.   How is sexual orientation and heterosexuality discussed across these two forums?

6.   *Gender and Non-Heterosexual Experiences*

Use InfoTrac to find the following article entitled "Sexual Identity Trajectories among Sexual-Minority Youths: Gender Comparisons" by R. C. Savin-Williams and L. Diamond in *Archives of Sexual Behavior*, December 2000.

a.   How do men and women differ in the way they develop their sexual orientation identity?

b.   How might understanding this difference help develop support for gay youth and lesbians?

7.   *Sexual Orientation in the Schools*

Students in high schools across the United States are beginning to appreciate the benefits of forming gay / lesbian / bi/ transgender / straight alliances. These are groups that share information and support for all students in dealing with sexuality and sexual identity, including sexual orientation.

Research suggests that most young people, both gay and straight, know or have a sense of their sexual orientation much earlier than high school, at around age 9. Do you think parents, teachers, and others need to make an effort to provide information and support to children at this age?

Using InfoTrac, search for information about parents, teachers, counselors, and others concerned about this issue.

a.   What possible interventions do they suggest?

b.   What makes interventions controversial?

c.   How is the solution to this concern linked to sex education in the schools? How is the solution to this concern linked to education regarding diversity and families? Does a discussion of sexual orientation have to include a discussion of sex?

8.   Sexual Orientation and Coming Out

Using InfoTrac, search for articles related to **coming out**. Choose several articles and discuss the following:

a.   How is the term coming out being used in the articles? In what ways do non-heterosexually identified individuals "come out" (to self, to family, to friends, to faith communities, to co-workers, etc.)? Can anyone ever be completely out?

b.   What challenges face individuals regarding coming out? What are the social and psychological consequences (both positive and negative)?

c.   Is there a comparable coming out experience for heterosexual individuals? How do heterosexual individuals inform others of their sexual orientation identity? What are the social and psychological consequences of making a heterosexual identity known in a social context?

9.   Understanding Bisexuality

Using InfoTrac, search key terms **bisexual** and **bisexuality** to locate the article "Living Life in the Double Closet: Bisexual Youth Speak Out" by K. McLean in *Hecate*, May 2001.

a.   What issues do the participants raise regarding their bisexual identities?

b.   In what ways do the experiences of the participants challenge the stereotypes of bisexuality?

c.   How do the experiences of bisexual individuals differ from those that identify as gay or lesbian?

## 10.	Homophobia and Hate Crimes

What social factors cause homophobia that may lead to prejudice, discrimination, and even hate crimes against gay, lesbian, bisexual, or transgender individuals or groups?

Read about one of the following issues or incidents that reflect homophobia in our society. They include both real events, their fictional retellings, and related issues.

- The murder of Matthew Sheppard

- The "gay panic" defense

- Hate-crime legislation

- "Boys Don't Cry" (1999 film)

Describe the case or story. Then discuss how your choice reflects homophobia and how it has influenced (increased or diminished) homophobia. Explain.

## 11.	Lesbian, Gay, Bisexual, and Transgender Politics

While not as obvious or dramatic as physical violence, the damage done by denying civil rights to non-heterosexuals is a fundamental concern of the LGBT community. Choose one of the following topics and explore its related civil rights controversies.

- Boy Scouts
- Don't Ask, Don't Tell (military politics)
- Job discrimination (teachers, coaches, etc.)
- Partnership rights (the right to marry or form legal or religious unions)

Then compare progress nationally with the current situation in your state or city. Is your community a leader in LGBT rights? Explain why or why not.

12.   Civil Unions and Marriages

Using InfoTrac, search the key terms **civil unions, domestic partnerships,** and **gay marriage**. Find and read 5-10 articles on the topic, then answer the following:

   a.   How would you characterize the arguments used for and against the legal recognition of same-sex relationships? Are there certain groups of individuals that are more likely to support / not support legal recognition of same-sex relationships?

   b.   How do arguments from advocates for civil unions differ from arguments from advocates of gay marriage?

   c.   In what way is the issue of gay marriage a human rights issue? How is it similar to or different from other civil rights movements?

   d.   How is the issue of legal recognition of same-sex relationships relevant to the issues listed below? What other issues are relevant to the topic?

   - Religious beliefs
   - Heterosexual privilege
   - Civil rights
   - Parenting rights
   - Medical insurance
   - Living will
   - Tax benefits
   - Discrimination
   - Family

Chapter 11

Contraception

1.   *Contraceptive Methods*

Using InfoTrac, investigate methods of **contraception** people have used in other times. To narrow your search, use the key term **history and contraception**.

      a.   List two contraceptive methods that are no longer used today in the United States.

      b.   What similarities do they share with current methods?

      c.   What is the most common contraceptive method in use around the world today?

Look up contraception and the name of a country or culture of your choice. Then discuss the following:

      d.   Do women and men in this society have access to a safe and effective form of contraception? Why or why not? What are some of the obstacles that sexually active adults and adolescents face in obtaining the contraception they need?

      e.   How does their system compare with that in the United States?

2.   *Controlling Contraception Information*

In the early twentieth century, Margaret Sanger defied the **Comstock Laws** to get contraception information and devices to women.

What are some of the controls or limitations on information that are still in effect in the United States today? These may include formal laws or less formal social restrictions, or controls that make gaining contraception or birth control information difficult.

Name one and discuss its effect. With what intent is the control imposed? Is the source of control religion, the government, or other factors?

3. Pioneers in Contraception

On InfoTrac, search information on an individual (such as **Margaret Sanger**) or organization (such as **Planned Parenthood Federation of America**) that has worked to make contraception accessible and safe.

Then consider for your choice:

a. What was the precipitating event or cause that led this pioneer to focus on family planning?

b. What obstacles stood in the way?

c. What degree of public acceptance did this pioneer receive? From what sectors of society?

d. What is the lasting accomplishment of this pioneer (how has contraceptive practice changed in the United States as a result of the efforts made)?

e. Do any of the obstacles faced by the pioneer still remain in place today?

4. Gendered Perspectives on Contraception

Using InfoTrac, search key terms **women and contraception, men and contraception**. Compare the search results in order to think about ways in which issues of contraception are framed similarly or differently for women and men.

a. Did each search yield similar results? Discuss the relative number of articles for each search, as well as any similarities or differences across the content of the articles.

Choose one article that is relevant to male contraception and one that is relevant to female contraception. For each discuss the following:

b. How is interest in, and responsibility for, contraception considered?

c. Who is the audience for each of the articles? How is the issue of contraception represented across gender, race/ethnicity, social class, age, religious identity, and other variables?

d. Do you feel that issues of contraception are presented, researched, and practiced in comparable ways for men and women? Why or why not?

5. Abstinence and Contraception

Abstinence and methods based on the menstrual cycle are the only contraceptive methods that receive official approval of the **Catholic Church**. In 2001, the church offered updated guidelines about **contraception**. Using InfoTrac, explore this topic, and then consider the following:

a. Briefly describe the Catholic Church's current position on contraception.

b. Do most U.S. Catholics follow the Vatican's guidelines?

c. Are there indications that the Catholic Church will modify its position given the views of church members?

6. The Day-After Pill

It was a clinic secret for decades. Now some health providers want to make the **day-after (or morning-after) pill** available at pharmacies without prescription. Read about the combination of pills that can prevent pregnancy if taken up to 72 hours after unprotected vaginal intercourse. Based on your reading discuss the following:

a. Who is most likely to use this type of contraception?

b. Which social groups oppose its use? Why?

c. Is there evidence that some women use this method as their only contraception?

d. Is it likely that this method will be approved in the United States as an over-the-counter contraceptive? Why or why not?

7. Religion and Contraception: A Case Study

Using InfoTrac, use the key term **emergency contraception** to locate the following article: "Pharmacist's Refusal to Fill Emergency Contraception Script Raises Questions" from *Drug Week*, March 2004. Read the article and answer the following questions:

a. What was the controversy discussed in the article?

b. What were the responses of pro-choice individuals and pro-life individuals to this case?

c. How are issues of contraception related to the issue of abortion?

d. Is this case a good example of the stance taken by pro-life and pro-choice supporters? Why or why not?

8.   Contraception, Abortion and Infanticide

Access to reliable and safe contraception is a way to keep abortion rates low. In some societies, good contraception policy may even help prevent infanticide.

Using InfoTrac, find out which countries have high rates of **abortion** and **infanticide**. Pick one country. Then, for that country consider the following:

      a.   Do women have access to birth control? If so, what kind?

      b.   What efforts are being made by governments, international organizations or women's groups to change the situation?

      c.   Are there societies where one sex is more often subject to infanticide? Why?

      d.   Are there any aspects of the country's situation that resemble that of the United States?

9.   Comparing Contraceptive Methods

Your text lists hormonal, barrier, and intrauterine methods of birth control. Many of these are quite good, yet there is not yet a perfect contraceptive: one that is reliable, has no risks or side effects, and actually enhances sex.

Consider current research on new **contraceptive methods**.

Find one example of research that might lead to a new, improved birth control method, procedure, or device. Describe the following:

      a.   Who would use it?

      b.   How does it improve on existing methods?

      c.   What are the drawbacks to this method?

10. Contraception Controversies

There are many troubling chapters in the history of contraception. Some of the worst are tests or marketing of contraceptive methods on women that were not safe, and the unauthorized medical sterilization of women as a type of social engineering.

Examine the history of an incident of your choice or one of the following:

- **Contraceptive testing** by the United States in Puerto Rico and other countries

- The **Dalkon Shield** suit

- **Sterilization** of socially disadvantaged women without their knowledge

Then discuss the following:

a.   Which women were affected?

b.   Was there redress for their injuries?

c.   Are laws now in place that insure that similar tragedies will not occur in the future?

11. Contraception Across the Life Span

Using InfoTrac, search the following key terms: **teenagers and contraception, adults and contraception, marriage and contraception.** Then discuss the following:

a.   How is contraception discussed similarly and differently during adolescence and adulthood?

b.   In the articles generated from the **adults and contraception** search, are there some groups of adults that are focused on more frequently? If yes, why do you think this is the case?

c.   How does the discussion of contraception differ for married and unmarried populations?

d.   In what ways is contraception discussed as a means of preventing conception? In what ways is contraception discussed as a means of preventing sexually transmitted diseases? As reflected in your searches, how does the focus of contraception change across the life span?

12. *Contraception and Sexuality: Thinking About Research Methods*

Using InfoTrac, locate the article "Sexual Knowledge, Attitudes, and Risk Behaviors of Students in Turkey" in *Journal of School Health*, September 2003. Read the article and then answer the following questions.

a.   In general, what was the purpose of the study?

b.   How does the issue of contraception relate to the stated purpose of the study?

c.   How were risk behaviors operationalized / measured in the research study?

d.   Who were the participants in the study? Describe participant characteristics including age, sex, sexual orientation, and religion. Note what characteristics are known to the reader and what information you might still like to know about the participants.

e.   What were the main findings of the research?

f.   Do you find the research believable? To what group or groups do you think the research findings relate? Why?

Chapter 12

Conceiving Children: Process and Choice

1.   Infertility

It is not uncommon in the United States today to remain "childless by choice." However, people who want biological children and have been unable to conceive can feel as if the choice was not theirs to make. Although the causes of infertility are not fully understood, there are some social behaviors that are thought to contribute to making conception less likely.

Using InfoTrac, search the key term **infertility.** Then discuss the following:

   a.   Does research show that infertility is truly on the rise, or is it impossible to know? Explain your answer.

   b.   Discuss the effect on fertility for each of the following:
   - **STDs**
   - **Age**
   - **Alcohol, drug use, and smoking**
   - **Environmental factors**

2.   Reproductive Technologies

Using InfoTrac, explore some of the techniques that are helping some infertile couples to conceive a child. Then discuss the following questions:

   a.   Which is least invasive?

   b.   Which method(s) uses the mother's gametes but not her partner's?

   c.   Which method(s) uses the father's gametes but not the mother's?

   d.   Is there a method that uses neither the future mother's nor the future father's gametes but allows a mother to give birth?

Examine one case of **surrogate motherhood**. Describe the case from three perspectives: the surrogate mother, the genetic mother, and the father. (Make note of whether or not the father is the genetic parent.) What is the status of the following new technologies?

   - **Gene therapy to avoid health problems in offspring**

   - **Artificial womb**

3. *Gendered Perspectives on Fertility and Reproduction*

Using InfoTrac, search the following key terms: **women and fertility, men and fertility, women and reproduction, men and reproduction**. Compare the search results in order to think about ways in which issues of fertility and reproduction are framed similarly or differently for women and men.

a. Did each search yield similar results? Discuss the relative number of articles for each search, as well as any similarities or differences across the content of the articles.

Choose one article that is relevant to male fertility and reproduction and one that is relevant to female fertility and reproduction. For each discuss the following:

b. How is interest in, and responsibility for, reproduction considered?

c. Who is the audience for each of the articles? How is the issue represented across gender, race/ethnicity, social class, age, religious identity, and other variables?

d. Do you feel that issues of reproduction and fertility are presented, researched, and practiced in comparable ways for men and women? Why or why not?

4. *Reproductive Choice*

Elective abortion is, and is likely to remain, a controversial subject in American society and politics. Abortion was ignored by U.S. laws until the 1960s, when it was prohibited except to save a woman's life. From that time until 1972, women who wanted to end their pregnancies were forced to risk their health and sometimes their lives.

Using InfoTrac, examine the abortion controversy and compare the views of those who want to protect a woman's right to choose and those who believe that abortion is murder.

a. Summarize the perspectives of the two opposing sides.

b. List three ways in which opponents of choice have sought to end or limit access to abortion services and/or to change the law to prohibit them.

c. List three things that activists for choice have done to protect women's reproductive rights.

d. Do you think that it is accurate to consider the abortion issue as having two opposing sides? Why or why not? Do you think there are more than two ways of conceptualizing the abortion debate?

e.   Compare the U.S. controversy with that of a single European country. Is abortion at the center of their elective politics, as it is in the United States? Do most citizens of that country support a woman's right to choose or do they wish to outlaw or strictly limit access to abortion services?

5.   *Understanding the Abortion Debate: Where Do You Stand?*

Using InfoTrac, search key term **abortion** to identify articles from various perspectives. Then consider the following:

a.   Before reading the articles, briefly summarize your thinking on abortion. What are your reasons for holding this view?

b.   Choose several articles and briefly summarize the main arguments highlighted by each source.

c.   How did each source support the arguments made? (legal and/or moral arguments, research findings, images, etc.)

d.   How were these arguments addressed/countered by other sources?

e.   What is the language used to discuss abortion? Using InfoTrac search different key terms: **abortion rights, anti-abortion, anti-choice, anti-life, reproductive rights, right to life,** etc. Who is most likely to use each of these terms? How does the language used in discussing the topic of abortion affect your perception of the issue?

f.   Did reading the articles lead you to change your initial position on abortion?

g.   What other information would you like to better support your position?

6.   *Childbirth Options*

A woman's experience of childbirth is never predictable. Women do have some say, however, about who will attend the birth of their child.

At one time midwives delivered all children. Today physicians deliver most. Yet a growing number of women whose pregnancies are without complications are opting for the less interventionist approach of midwives.

Using InfoTrac, examine some of the controversies surrounding the use of **midwives**. Write a brief status report on midwifery in the United States that addresses the following:

a. What is the certification or training for midwives in the United States?

b. How are midwives viewed by physicians and nurses?

c. What are the differences between certified nurse midwives (CNMs) and other (lay) midwives?

d. Why do some women prefer midwives?

e. What do you think will be the future of midwifery in the United States?

7. *Medical Interventions During Childbirth*

Using InfoTrac, search articles to understand the pros and cons of different medical interventions during childbirth. Choose one of the following medical interventions and relate the current issues surrounding this practice.

- **Medications**
- **Episiotomy**
- **Forceps / Vacuum extraction**
- **Cesarean section**

Then discuss the following questions:

a. How readily is this intervention used in the United States? How does this compare to other countries?

b. Who makes the decision regarding whether the intervention is necessary or administered?

c. What are the risks involved?

d. Under what circumstances is the intervention beneficial?

e. What current debates exist regarding the intervention?

8. *Fathers and Fertility*

Using InfoTrac, search for information on the significance of a father's age and health on fertility. What are some of the ways a father influences his offspring's health?

Then discuss: What do you think of men in their 70s and beyond fathering biological children? How does women's inability to have biological children after menopause affect sexual relations between the genders?

9. The Rights of Mother and Fetus

Using InfoTrac, search **mother and fetus**. Find information on a legal case in which a mother is accused of harming her unborn child because of drug or alcohol use, smoking, or other circumstances.

Write a brief summary of the case. For your summary, consider the following:

a. What are the concerns for the fetus?

b. What rights of the mother are at issue?

c. What is your opinion about the intervention of medical or legal authorities in a woman's pregnancy? Who should determine when it is justified or necessary?

10. Reproductive Implications: The Impact of Technology

Recent development in fertility technology has led to new considerations for parenting. Using InfoTrac, search the following key terms: **fertility, fertility and parenting, age and parenting, sperm bank, fertility and sex of child**. Using the articles from your search consider the following:

a. Describe some of the issues regarding fertility and parenting that have surfaced with new reproductive technologies.

b. What methods have led to these new concerns?

c. Who is most likely to benefit from these new technologies? For example, does everyone have equal access to these methods? If not, why?

11. *Considering the Source: Sperm Bank*

Using InfoTrac, locate three articles on the topic of **sperm banks**. Read the articles and answer the following questions:

a. What are the different reasons that lead individuals to rely upon sperm banks for fertility options?

b. What specific social and legal issues are related to the use of sperm banks?

c. Who is most likely to use a sperm bank option?

d. What concerns or questions would you have regarding using a sperm donor for reproduction? How might these concerns differ for men and women?

12. *Reproductive Ethics*

Using InfoTrac, search key term **reproductive ethics**. Read several articles and consider the following questions:

a. What ethical issues are raised in the article?

b. How are these issues framed with regard to individual freedom?

c. How are ethical concerns of reproduction related to the following?

- Parent-child relationships
- Mother and father responsibility
- Religion
- Parental rights
- Rights of the fetus
- Medical risk

Chapter 13

Sexuality During Childhood and Adolescence

1.   Are Infants Sexual?

Your text describes observations made by parents (and noted by Kinsey) of sexual behavior in very young children. Using InfoTrac, find recent research on infant sexuality. Then discuss the following questions:

   a.   Of what kind of sexual behavior are infants capable?

   b.   How do experts recommend that parents respond to this behavior when it occurs?

   c.   Why do you think many adults are uncomfortable with infant sexuality? How does this reflect societal beliefs about sexuality and human nature?

2.   Childhood Sexuality and Sexual Play

Half to three-quarters of children engage in sexual play. Studies have found that sexual behavior such as **self-stimulation, exhibitionism,** and rubbing against another person often occurs among children ages 2-12.

Nearly everyone can remember seeing or engaging in this kind of behavior as a child. In your experience, what was the reaction of parents or other adults when they witnessed this sort of behavior? Describe what the adult did or said and how the children reacted.

What does that parental response reflect about our society's sexual beliefs? What message does it give to the child?

Compare your observations with the suggestion of sex researchers. Using InfoTrac, read recent research on **childhood sexuality** and see what experts advise to help foster healthful sexual attitudes in children.

71

3. *Children and Sex in Other Societies*

Some societies are openly accepting of sexual behavior in children and adolescents. Consider the **Mangaia, Trobriand Islanders, Lepcha, Romonum Islanders, Marquesas** or another society of your choice. Then answer the following questions:

    a.   How do parents respond to the sexual play of children?

    b.   How do children learn about sexuality? Who teaches them and in what setting or context?

    c.   What is the relation between the sexuality of children and that of adults in the same society?

4. *Reading the Research on Sexual Experiences in Childhood*

Using InfoTrac, use the search term **childhood sexuality** in order to locate the following article: "Sexual Experiences in Childhood: Young Adults' Recollections" in *Archives of Sexual Behavior*, June 2002.

Read the Introduction section of the article and then answer the following questions:

    a.   How has past research considered issues of childhood sexuality?

    b.   How does the current study approach the topic differently?

Read the Methods section of the article and then answer the following questions:

    c.   How would you describe the participants of the study?

    d.   How were the data collected? What types of questions were asked?

Read the Results and Discussion sections of the study and then answer the following questions:

    e.   What were the main findings of the study?

    f.   How did the authors explain the results?

    g.   What methodological considerations did they discuss when interpreting the results?

    h.   What questions remain regarding childhood sexuality? What should future research address?

5.   *Is Puberty Starting Earlier?*

Read some of the recent studies showing that girls, especially, are beginning to develop secondary sexual characteristics at ages 7, 8, and 9, several years before they begin menstruation at the average age of 11.

a.   What is the evidence for this early development?

b.   What are some of the theories as to why this is occurring in the United States? Consider dietary changes, social influences, pheromones, and environmental factors.

c.   What is the influence of the media in encouraging children to self-impose gender-specific behaviors?

d.   Do you think sex education needs to be taught in the 2nd and 3rd grades? Why or why not?

6.   *Teen Sexuality*

Is sexuality during adolescence less confusing and contradictory than a generation ago? Using InfoTrac, search the key term **teen sexuality** and consider one of the following issues:

a.   The Double Standard: Does our society accept sexual activity equally in teenage girls and boys? Does the term "slut" still have a meaning that "stud" does not? Or are these terms no longer heard?

b.   What are the issues that gay, lesbian, and bisexual teens face in adolescence? Are there signs that heterosexually minded schools and families have adapted to meet the needs of sexual minority youth?

c.   What special challenges do boys face at adolescence, when they still may be physically less mature than the girls their age? Consider the images of macho masculinity that boys may try to emulate.

7.   *Health Sexuality During the Teen Years*

Using InfoTrac, find out what researchers have learned about the most effective way to ensure sexual health among teens. Choose one of the following topics and answer the accompanying questions:

a.   Which environment is more likely to have a high rate of teen pregnancy: One where teens can talk with peers and adults about their sexual concerns? Or one where sex is treated as if it did not exist?

b.   Many young women and some young men experience unwanted sex during their teen years. Some experience rape. What can parents, educators, and health professionals do to reduce the rate of sexual violence among teens?

c.   What are the consequences of making condoms available to teens? Does it promote sexual activity that would not have taken place otherwise? Does it relate to a lower rate of STDs among teens? Check out the study that compared the New York high schools districts that made condoms available to high schools in Chicago that did not make them available. What were the relative rates of sexual activity?

d.   What evidence is there that teens are taking precautions to protect themselves from STDs? What kind of information and resources do teens need to help avoid unsafe sex?

8.   *Teen Pregnancy*

Rates of **teen pregnancy** have been dropping in the United States over the past decade. Find two articles that discuss this finding and indicate possible explanations for this shift.

Despite the drop, the United States still has higher teen birth rates than any other industrialized country. What are the societal, governmental, or other reasons why the U.S. rates are so high?

9.   *Sexuality Research: Approaches in Childhood and Adolescence*

In general, researching sexual topics poses methodological challenges. Researching these topics in childhood and adolescence poses even greater challenges. Using InfoTrac, locate articles utilizing the following search terms: **childhood and sexuality, adolescence and sexuality, adult sexuality**. Limit this search in InfoTrac by checking the box to consider only referred publications. Then consider how issues of sexuality are researched differently across childhood and adolescence:

a.   Are there an equal number of articles found for each search (childhood, adolescence, adulthood)?

b.   How are the topics researched during each life stage similar or different?

c.   What methods of data collection are used in the research (surveys, interviews, medical records, etc.)? How does the methodology change across the life stage studied?

d.   What special considerations do researchers need to make when studying sexuality in childhood? How are these similar to or different from considerations made when studying sexuality in adolescence?

10. *Sexual Orientation and Adolescence*

Using InfoTrac, locate articles using the key terms **sexual orientation and adolescence, sexual orientation and youth,** and **sexual orientation**. Choose one of the following issues on which to focus, then answers the questions below:

- **Sexual orientation disclosure or coming out**
- **"Passing"**
- **Same-sex friendships**
- **Physical and sexual abuse**
- **Dating and romantic relationships**
- **Sexual behavior**
- **Religion**
- **Drug abuse**
- **Homophobia / bullying / discrimination**
- **Relationship with parents**

a. How are issues of sexual orientation discussed in the context of adolescence? How are they discussed similarly and differently for adolescent and adult populations?

b. How are these issues discussed differently for heterosexual and non-heterosexual youth?

c. How are these issues discussed across gender (male / female) and across sexual orientation identity (gay / lesbian / bisexual / heterosexual)?

11.   *Focusing on Sexual Experiences in Adolescence*

Using InfoTrac, locate articles using the key terms **sexuality, sexuality and youth,** and **sexuality and adolescence**. Choose one of the following issues and then answer the questions below:

- **Sexual consent**
- **Safe-sex**
- **Virginity and abstinence**
- **Physical and sexual abuse**
- **Love and sexuality**
- **Sexual behavior**
- **Sexuality and religion**
- **Sexuality and drug abuse**
- **Sexual orientation**
- **Masturbation**
- **Contraception**

a.   How are issues of sexuality discussed in the context of adolescence? How are they discussed similarly and differently for adolescent and adult populations?

b.   How are these issues discussed differently for heterosexual and non-heterosexual youth?

c.   How are these issues discussed across gender (male / female) and across ethnic or racial identity?

d.   What special considerations do researchers make when investigating sexuality during adolescence?

12. Sex Education on the Internet: A Research Study

Using InfoTrac, locate the following article: "SexEd.com: Values and Norms in Web-based Sexuality Education" in *The Journal of Sex Research*, August 2001.

Read the Introduction and Methods sections of the article, and then answer the following:

a. According to the author, why might a Web-based sexuality education program be effective?

b. How does the author characterize school-based sexuality education (SBSE)?

c. How was the research conducted? What were the five hypotheses of the study? Choose one hypothesis that is most interesting to you.

At the end of the article, the Web sites used in the analysis are listed. Visit two of the Web sites.

d. Using your chosen hypothesis, determine whether it is supported based on the content of the Web sites you visited. Describe how the hypothesis is either supported or not supported.

Read the Results and Discussion sections of the article, and then answer the following:

e. Does the result of your analysis match that of the authors?

f. Ultimately, what do the authors conclude regarding the effectiveness of Web-based sexuality education?

g. Do you think Web-based sexuality education is more effective than school-based sexuality education? Why or why not?

Chapter 14

Sexuality and the Adult Years

1.   *Marriage in Global Perspective*

Marriage is an institution that takes many forms. In other societies, it can be a union of two families, while in the United States, most people see it as a union of two individuals. Those individuals pledge emotional and sexual exclusivity to their partner, are monogamous, and heterosexual. The union is legal, permanent, and often a religious bond.

Take any one of the above qualities and find a culture where that quality is not reflected in the experience of marriage. (For example, a polygamous society, or a country where marriage is extended not only to heterosexuals). Do you think our marriage and the other culture's unions are rightly called by the same name? What attributes do they share?

2.   *Legal Recognition of Same-Sex Partners / Same-Sex Marriage*

In 2000, the state of Vermont became the first to recognize same-sex couples for **civil unions,** and **gay marriage** became available in the Netherlands. In May 2004, Massachusetts will allow the first same-sex marriages in the United States. Yet elsewhere laws are passed to restrict the civil rights of gays and lesbians, including the right to marry.

Using InfoTrac, find out about one of the places where same-sex marriage is legal or where it is in the process of becoming legal. Then answer the following:

a.   Who is providing the impetus for this change?

b.   Is the change universally welcomed by the gay and lesbian communities? Why do some oppose the movement to legalize marriage?

c.   Do you foresee a day when every U.S. state allows gay civil unions or marriages? Why or why not? What are the remaining obstacles?

3. *Research on Same-Sex Relationships: Where Does the Question of Marriage Fit In?*

Using InfoTrac, conduct two searches using the key terms **same-sex relationships** or **same-sex marriage**. First, conduct an open search of all InfoTrac sources. Second, conduct a limited search of referred publications only.

a. Answer the following questions by comparing results across the two searches: Were the same topics addressed? How was the information presented similarly and differently for the two audiences?

b. Answer the following questions by focusing on the research articles only: How are same-sex relationships discussed? What research is available that may be relevant to the current debate on same-sex marriages? Consider research on the following topics:

- Lesbian, gay, and bisexual individuals as parents
- Relationship satisfaction in nonheterosexual relationships
- Longevity of nonheterosexual relationships
- Effect of discrimination and stigma on relationships
- Heterosexism
- Factors influencing attitudes towards heterosexual marriage

c. What is your opinion of same-sex marriage? What research evidence supports your opinion? What additional information would you like to see on the topic? What should future research address in order to inform the debate on same-sex marriage?

4. *Marriage or the Single Life?*

Who enjoys sex more? Married couples or singles? Using InfoTrac, locate articles using the search terms **marriage and sexuality** and **marital satisfaction**.

a. What does research suggest about the relationship between marriage and sexual satisfaction?

b. What do we know about the relationship between marriage and sexual satisfaction later in life?

The 2000 census showed that more people than ever live alone. Using InfoTrac, find out how demographers explain the increase in the number of people living alone.

c. Do you think this increase in the number of **singles** means there is less support for marriage in our society? How does this trend relate to the phenomenon of serial monogamy?

80

5. Divorce and Serial Monogamy

With high rates of divorce, some consider the family form in the United States to be **serial monogamy.** Individuals have only one spouse at a time, but over a lifetime many individuals have more than one spouse. What do you think of this trend?

Using InfoTrac, locate articles on the topic and answer the following questions:

a. Does serial monogamy affect women and men equally? Does one sex have a greater chance of remarrying after divorce?

b. What is the impact (both positive and negative) of divorce and remarriage on children?

c. What do you think of efforts such as covenant marriage and other efforts to make divorce more difficult? Should the government intervene in this way? Why or why not?

6. Cultural notions of Marriage and Sexuality: A Case Study of Extramarital Sex in Contemporary Nigeria

Using InfoTrac, locate the article entitled "'Man No Be Wood': Gender and Extramarital Sex in Contemporary Southeastern Nigeria" in *Ahfad Journal*, December 2002. Read the article and then answer the following questions:

a. What research methods were used for this analysis? Do you think the method was a good one for the topic considered?

b. In general, how are extramarital affairs regarded by men and women in the Nigerian culture described?

c. How are women and men portrayed in the Nigerian culture studied? How do issues of class influence the way women and men are regarded? How is that similar or different from the way women and men are portrayed in the United States?

d. What are the unwritten "rules" regarding married men and their lovers?

e. How does learning about Nigerian culture influence the way you think about the topics of extramarital sex, gender roles, and marriage?

7. Cybersex, Pornography, and Relationships

Imagine discovering that your partner engages in erotic banter with another person online. Imagine your partner regularly visits pornographic Web sites. How would you feel? What would you do?

Using InfoTrac, look for accounts of how people are coping with Internet chat rooms, romances, infidelities, and more. Compare your hypothetical experience (above) with research evidence about the effect that virtual **cybersex** is having on actual couples and relationships.

8. Gender and the Double Standard

How does the double standard manifest itself in relationships? Put a plus or minus in the column under men and women indicating who is more or less likely to have this experience. Use InfoTrac to research the answers.

	Women	*Men*
Ease of finding a partner		
Being partnered in later life		
Remarrying after divorce		
Having an extramarital affair		
Being cared for by spouse when ill		

What do your results suggest about the different roles and expectations of women and men in marriage?

9. Covenant Marriage and Divorce

How can you explain the finding that states offering **covenant marriage** have higher divorce rates than those states that do not? Using InfoTrac, explore recent efforts to introduce covenant marriage. Choose one state that has introduced or passed this legislation, and answer the following:

    a.   What are the social factors that inspired the legislation?

    b.   Who introduced the legislation? Why?

    c.   Has the program proven effective in reducing the divorce rate? Why or why not?

10. *Focusing on Sexual Experiences Later in Life*

Using InfoTrac, locate articles using key terms **sexuality, sexuality and aging,** and **sexuality and elderly**. Choose one of the following issues to focus on, and then answer the questions below:

- **Sexual consent**
- **Safe-sex, STDs, and AIDS**
- **Virginity**
- **Physical and sexual abuse**
- **Love and sexuality**
- **Extramarital affairs**
- **Marital status and widowhood**
- **Sexual behavior**
- **Nonsexual friendships**
- **Sexuality and religion**
- **Sexuality and drug abuse**
- **Sexual orientation**
- **Masturbation**
- **Contraception**
- **Sexual health**

a. How are issues of sexuality discussed in the context of aging? How are they discussed similarly and differently across the adult life cycle (early adulthood, midlife, later life)?

b. How are these issues discussed differently for heterosexual and non-heterosexual individuals in elderly populations?

c. How are these issues discussed across gender (male / female) and across ethnic or racial identity?

d. What special considerations do researchers make when investigating sexuality and aging?

e. How might stereotypes regarding sexuality and aging affect the way sexuality research in aging populations is framed?

11. Interracial Dating and Marriage

Using InfoTrac, review recent research on **interracial dating** and **interracial marriage**. Then answer the following questions:

a. What are the current themes in research on the topic of interracial dating? What are the potential obstacles that interracial couples face?

b. What is the history of the legal status of interracial marriage in the United States?

c. How do interracial marriage rates differ across ethnic / racial communities? What accounts for the differences?

d. How are issues of interracial marriage similar to or different from issues of same-sex marriage in the United States? How has the legal system responded similarly or differently to the two marriage issues?

12. Mail-Order Brides Meet E-Mail

Using InfoTrac, locate the article entitled "E-Brides: the Mail-order Bride Industry and the Internet" in *Canadian Woman Studies*, Spring-Summer, 2003. Read the article, and then answer the following questions:

a. Summarize the description of the internet mail-order bride industry.

b. Why do you think that women from certain countries (such as the Philippines and other Asian countries) are more likely to be utilized in this market?

c. How do issues of sex, race, and class relate to the mail-order bride industry?

d. What do you feel mail-order bride markets reflect about the way in which marriage is regarded? What does the existence of this market reflect about the way women's roles in relationships are viewed in U.S. culture?

Chapter 15

The Nature and Origin of Sexual Difficulties

1. Sexual Difficulties and Illness or Disability

Illness and disability can impair sexual function. Yet regaining the ability to enjoy sex is considered an important part of recovery, treatment, or learning to live with a disability.

Recent research on spinal-cord injuries is particularly interesting because it also has improved our understanding of basic sexual function. Using InfoTrac, find articles on **spinal-cord injury and sexuality**, and then answer the following questions:

    a.   Why does spinal-cord injury affect sexual function?

    b.   Do we know more about this injury in women or in men?

    c.   Why do you think therapy for people with these injuries involves both physical and psychological treatment?

2. Sexual Difficulties Caused by Drug Use and Abuse

Sexual difficulties can be caused by the abuse of recreational drugs, including alcohol, tobacco, marijuana, cocaine, and amphetamines, as well as the use of certain widely used medicines such as anti-depressants and anti-hypertensive medications.

Two of the most commonly used drugs are alcohol and tobacco. Choose one of these and, using InfoTrac, consider the ways it affects sexual function. Then discuss the following:

    a.   What is the social context in which it seems acceptable to smoke or drink?

    b.   How does its use influence behavior?

    c.   What is the physical effect on the body that impairs sexuality?

    d.   What is not known about this drug's effect that still needs to be researched?

3. Sexual Difficulties with Social Causes

The double standard. Poor sex education. A narrow definition of sex. These are examples of social factors that can negatively affect sex for otherwise healthy adults. One of the most pernicious social factors is poor body image. Using InfoTrac, search the key term **body image and sexuality,** and then discuss the following:

a. Where do young women and men get their ideas about physical beauty?

b. Ideals of beauty have typically affect women more than men. Do you think men are just as vulnerable today? Provide evidence in support of your answer.

c. Are there different ideals of beauty among U.S. subcultures? Provide examples.

d. Do you think beauty ideals can be changed to be more inclusive? Do you think changing our ideal can improve sexual health?

4. Sexual Function Problems and Gender

Using InfoTrac, locate the following article: "Sexual Function Problems and Help Seeking Behaviour in Britain: National Probability Sample Survey" in *British Medical Journal*, August 2003. Read the article and answer the following questions:

a. What was the purpose of the study?

b. What methods were used for data collection? Who were the participants in the study?

c. In what ways were the sexual function profiles for men and women similar or different?

d. Can you be sure that the results reflect gender differences in the frequency of sexual function problems? What other possible explanations could account for these results?

5.   *Women and Low Sexual Desire*

The most common reason women seek sexual help is because of lack of **sexual desire** or **sexual interest**. Researchers call it **hypoactive sexual desire disorder** and it is a problem that affects millions of people.

Using InfoTrac, research this topic. Then fill in the following chart with a list of possible physical or social causes. One example is given for each:

PHYSICAL   *SOCIAL / PSYCHOLOGICAL*

high blood pressure medicine   past experience of sexual abuse

6.   *Men's Most Common Sexual Concerns*

What is men's most common complaint regarding their sexual function? One might say that it is some aspect of "performance": gaining and maintaining an erection and timing orgasm and ejaculation.

Using InfoTrac, search **erectile dysfunction** and **premature ejaculation**. For each, find out:

a.   What health conditions can cause this problem?

b.   What are some recent treatments? How effective are they? Consider how they are related. Does ejaculation always occur with orgasm, or are they separate? Does erection always lead to ejaculation?

87

7. *The Orgasm Gap*

Though women do not always complain about it, many do not necessarily have an orgasm during sex. How can you explain why heterosexual sex almost always includes a man's orgasm, but not necessarily a woman's?

Use InfoTrac to explore **women and orgasm**. Then discuss the following:

      a.   Are women naturally less able to have orgasms than men? Why or why not?

      b.   What can women do to increase the likelihood of an orgasm in sex?

      c.   What can a woman's partner do to increase the likelihood of an orgasm?

8. *Researching Sexual Difficulties*

Using InfoTrac, find articles related to **sexual difficulties** or **sexual dysfunction**. Then consider the following:

      a.   Discuss some of the ways sexual difficulty or dysfunction is measured in research studies.

      b.   On which populations and under what circumstances do sexual dysfunction researchers usually focus?

      c.   How is sexual dysfunction considered similarly or differently across gender, race/ethnicity, class, and sexual orientation?

9. *Sexual Difficulties and Aging*

Using InfoTrac, locate the article "Aging and Sexuality" in *The Western Journal of Medicine*, October 1997. Read the article and then answer the following questions:

      a.   What is the myth regarding aging and sexuality dysfunction? What contributes to this myth?

      b.   How are issues of sexuality and aging discussed for men and women?

      c.   What are the key areas of sexual difficulties discussed in the article?

Chapter 16

Sexual Therapy and Enhancement

1. Sex Information: Books and Manuals

If an individual or couple wants a better sex life, where can they turn? Before seeking out a therapist, most look for information in **sex manuals**. How much do you know about this book genre?

Use sources from InfoTrac in order to answer *True* or *False* on the following questions:

a. The first sex manual was *The Joy of Sex*, written in the late 1960s.

b. As long as it is written by a doctor, all sex manuals will contain the same information.

c. *Becoming Orgasmic* is a sex manual for men.

d. In the United States, there is no stigma to perusing or purchasing a sex manual. (You are comfortable if you run into a friend in the sex section of your local bookstore).

2. Meeting Sexual Expectations

The media and the lack of good sex education sometimes leads women and men to have unrealistic ideas about what to expect from sex. For example, films show women who sound and look a certain way when they have an orgasm; men are expected to be ever aroused and ready for sex; women have orgasms from a rapid interlude of intercourse; couples enjoy simultaneous orgasms. Using InfoTrac, see what researchers have found about the **effects of sex in mass media** on people's sexual practices and satisfaction.

Write a brief summary of your findings. You might want to discuss the role of some of the following issues:

- Images of beauty
- Quality of sex information in media
- Degree of explicitness in sexual behavior
- Safer sex practices
- Double standard
- Unrealistic portrayals of sexual activity

3. *Enhancing Sex*

Some people enjoy their sex lives but want to learn and experience more – stronger or more frequent orgasms, a more encompassing physical or spiritual experience in sex or simply to try something new. On InfoTrac, search one of the following and then answer the questions below:

- **Tantric sex**
- **Sex toys**
- **Personals**
- **Cybersex**
- **Erotica**
- **Aphrodisiacs**
- **Instructional videos**
- **Sex surrogate**
- **Pornography**

a. Who uses and who benefits from the use of the resource you chose?

b. Do you think it is legitimate and valuable?

c. Does it complement or contradict traditional sex therapy? Explain your answer.

4. *Lasting Longer*

Premature ejaculation is one of the most common concerns of men about their sex lives. Explore InfoTrac for articles from journals and magazines that offer techniques to help men maintain an erection longer before ejaculation. Then answer the following:

a. Provide and define one common technique to address premature ejaculation.

b. Describe one mental exercise or technique men can use.

c. Give one piece of advice for a man's partner. How can he/she help?

d. What are some of the reasons that premature ejaculation is such a common problem?

5.   *Viagra*

Viagra and similar drugs have helped men with **erectile dysfunction**. Now many otherwise healthy men desire the drug to improve the length and quality of sex. Does Viagra represent a boon for sex in America or could it lead to a possibly dangerous or undesirable trend? Explore this trend on InfoTrac and then respond to the following:

   a.   Name two possible complications related to Viagra.

   b.   What are some medical conditions that can cause erectile dysfunction?

   c.   Do men's partners necessarily share the excitement about Viagra? Why or why not?

   d.   Why are some women's groups upset about the ease of availability of Viagra?

6.   *Treatments for Low Sexual Desire in Women*

What treatment options are available for women who have **hypoactive sexual desire disorder**? Using InfoTrac, search **sexual excitement, women and sexuality,** or other relevant terms. Then answer the following:

   a.   Are the main sources of women's sexual disinterest thought to be psychological or physiological? Why?

   b.   What are some suggestions for treatment for hypoactive sexual desire disorder from the popular press? From professional journals?

   c.   From your reading, what types of social factors are thought to be influences on women's level of sexual desire?

   d.   From your reading, do you think women can benefit from medical solutions (such as testosterone) even if the causes are psychological and social? Why or why not?

7. *Adult Sexuality and Childhood Victims of Sexual Abuse*

Physical or emotional trauma or abuse, including sexual abuse, can have profound consequences on many aspects of an individual's life, including sexuality.

Using InfoTrac, locate articles on **adult child sexual abuse victims**. Then answer the following questions:

a. Approximately what percentage of the female population has experienced some form of sexual abuse? What percentage of males?

b. What is the most common suggestion for addressing sexual problems for this population?

c. What social movements or public education efforts have been made to prevent child sexual abuse? What more needs to be done? Who should provide these services?

d. What role do you think the media can play in addressing this problem?

8. *Management of Vaginismus and Dyspareunia*

Using InfoTrac, locate the article entitled "Management of Dyspareunia and Vaginismus" in *American Family Physician*, April 2000. Read the article and answer the following questions:

a. How are vaginismus and dyspareunia defined in the article?

b. How does the author establish the importance of considering vaginismus and dyspareunia?

c. In what ways does the article discuss the physical, psychological, and social implications for vaginismus and dyspareunia?

9. Sexual Difficulties and Treatment

Imagine experiencing sexual difficulties. Who would you turn to for help and support? Would you feel comfortable discussing this with your partner, your friends, or your physician? How long would the difficultly exist before you would seek help? If your partner were experiencing the difficulties, would you be more or less ready to discuss the situation and seek help? Use InfoTrac to locate articles regarding **treatment and sexual difficulties**, and then answer the following questions:

a. When individuals seek help for sexual difficulties, where do they first turn?

b. How do psychologists, psychiatrists, and physicians differ in their approach to treating sexual difficulties? Is there reason to believe that some individuals feel more comfortable going to a certain type of professional for issues of sexual difficulties?

Chapter 17

Sexually Transmitted Diseases

1. *Self-Assessment: How Much Do You Know About STDs?*

Reading your chapter, you probably encountered STDs that are familiar to you. You may also have read about several that you had not heard of before. Pick one with which you are not familiar from the list below and search for additional information using InfoTrac.

- **Chlamydia**
- **Herpes**
- **HPV**
- **Gonorrhea**
- **Viral hepatitis**
- Or choose another STD

Then write a brief response using the questions below:

a. Why do you think you had not heard of this STD?

b. Is it an STD that is growing or diminishing in its prevalence?

c. Would your parents know about it? Would your same-sex or other-sex friends?

d. Will you talk to your friends and sexual partner(s) (if any) about this STD? Why or why not?

2. *The Risk of Various Sexual Activities*

Using InfoTrac, find out the risks for HIV transmission for each of the following behaviors:

- Oral sex on a woman
- Oral sex on a man
- Anal penetrative sex
- Vaginal penetrative sex
- Rimming

Using latex barriers lowers the risk of transmission. What conditions can *increase* a person's vulnerability?

3. Safer Sex Practices: When Latex is Not Enough

Herpes and **human papilloma virus** (HPV), two sexually transmitted viruses that can cause serious health problems, are not necessarily prevented by condoms even when used correctly. Using InfoTrac, research one of the two viruses and then consider the following:

    a.   What does the virus cause?

    b.   How widespread is the disease?

    c.   How is the virus spread?

    d.   Why are condoms not effective in preventing the spread of the virus?

    e.   What can a sexually active person do to minimize his/her risk of getting this virus?

4. HIV / AIDS

The **AIDS** pandemic is a worldwide health threat. Pick one of the following questions and explore this issue using InfoTrac.

    a.   Especially during the early years of the epidemic, AIDS activists had to resort to drastic measures to get some governments to pay attention to the disease. Why was this the case? Find information about the early 1980s in the United States and the efforts of groups such as **ACT UP**. Then explore what are the concerns of **AIDS activists** today.

    b.   What do researchers know so far about why some people carry the virus for AIDS but do not develop the disease? How might this phenomenon help lead to a vaccine? What kind of research is being done to find an AIDS vaccine?

    c.   What is the role of the U.S. government in ending the pandemic? Consider its efforts in the 1980s and those of today. Has the government's role in the fight against AIDS increased to a level that you feel is adequate? What role should the United States play in the AIDS struggles in Asia and Africa? (Use key terms **AIDS and Africa, AIDS in Asia, AIDS in the United States**)

5. HIV and Populations at Risk

Using InfoTrac, search for information on the **AIDS epidemic** in the U.S. Which subgroup of the population has the fastest growing rate of HIV infection? Write a paragraph explaining why this group became especially vulnerable. What aspects of their socioeconomic status have increased their risk? Consider the following factors:

- Income
- Age
- Ethnicity / Race
- Sexual orientation
- Status of partners / Behaviors of partners
- Access to health care
- Access to health education

6. Treatment Therapies, Vaccines, and HIV

Consider one of the major drug treatment and prevention strategies against AIDS. Use InfoTrac to search one of the following:

- Condoms
- Vaccines
- Antiretroviral and other drug therapies

For your selected term, answer the following questions:

a. How effective is this weapon against the spread of AIDS?

b. Is this approach the one likely to bring an end to AIDS? Will it help bring it under control?

c. What are the latest advances or developments regarding (your topic)?

d. What role does education play in the implementation of this approach? What possible stereotypes or misconceptions may act as obstacles?

e. Is this approach affordable and accessible to affected populations around the world? Why or why not?

7. Communication and Sexual Health

Your text emphasizes the importance of communication for sexual health. Consider the problem of communication about STDs at both the personal and the political levels.

Read the following and discuss whether you agree or not with each statement. Then, using InfoTrac, give an example from research articles to support your point of view.

a. When it comes to STDs, actions speak louder than words. You cannot rely on what your partner says about his or her past sexual activity. You should therefore always take the same precautions and use latex for safer sex.

b. The AIDS epidemic could have been slowed earlier if people were willing to talk about sex. (Just imagine if the disease had been transmitted via water rather than blood, semen, vaginal fluids, and breast milk! Would there have been a faster response?) Countries with more open approaches to sex (and less homophobia) started anti-AIDS campaigns early on and have lower infection rates.

8. STDs vs. Sexual Pleasure

Using InfoTrac, locate the article entitled "Many Men Would Rather Cope With STDs Than Use Condoms, Study Finds." in *Women's Health Weekly*, February 2004. Read the article and then answer the following questions:

a. What are the research findings under discussion in this article?

b. What were the reasons provided by men regarding why they did not use condoms regularly in their sexual relationships?

c. Who were the participants in the study? Do you feel that these participants are representative of most men? Why or why not?

d. This research report was published in *Women's Health Weekly*. Who do you think is the target audience for this research? What do you think is the intended outcome of publishing this research?

e. Do you think that if men or women read this article, that it might change their behavior in their sexual relationships? If yes, how?

9.   *STDs: A Hidden Epidemic*

Using InfoTrac, locate the article entitled "Confronting a Hidden Epidemic: The Institute of Medicine's Report on Sexually Transmitted Diseases" in *Family Planning Perspectives*, April 1997. Read the article and then answer the following questions:

a.   What are the main points under discussion in this article?

b.   Why does the article consider STDs to be a hidden epidemic? What evidence is used to support this characterization?

c.   What strategies were offered in the article to address this hidden epidemic? Do you think these strategies would be effective? Why or why not?

Chapter 18

Atypical Sexual Behavior

1.   Clarifying Terms

Using InfoTrac, search the following terms:

- **Fetishism**
- **Sadism**
- **Masochism**

For each, describe the following:

a.   What is the origin or root of the term?

b.   What is the current meaning of the term?

c.   Does our society pathologize this behavior or consider it harmless? Why?

2.   Survey

Using InfoTrac, search **voyeurism, exhibitionism, frotteurism,** and **obscene phone calls**. These are what your text calls "coercive paraphilias," atypical sexual behavior that is imposed on others without their consent.

Carry out a small survey among three women you know well, preferably women of different ages. Ask them if they have been at the receiving end of any of the above behaviors. You might want to also interview men to see if they have had these experiences.

Ask your interviewees to describe the behavior they witnessed and their reaction at the time. How did those behaviors make them feel? What do they think women should do to protect themselves from such behaviors? What can authorities do to reduce their incidence?

3. Exhibitionists and Voyeurs

Do we treat **exhibitionists** and voyeurs differently depending on gender? Do we view the performances of the men in "The Full Monty" or the Chippendales, whose audience is female, in the same way we do the much more plentiful instances of female performer and male viewer?

Using InfoTrac, search the terms **exhibitionism** and **voyeurism**. The first usually refers to a man who exposes himself to women without their consent. The second also typically refers to men who for sexual excitement observe women without their consent.

Compare these uses with the phenomenon of women who display themselves to a willing audience for money.

  a. Is agreeing to be viewed by others an exhibitionist act, similar to the stereotypical trench coat-wearing flasher? How is it similar or different?

  b. Is the audience that watches being voyeuristic? How are they different from a "peeping Tom"?

  c. Does this behavior depart from cultural convention, or is this so common that it might be considered "normal" in our society?

4. Gender, Technology and the Public Eye

Using InfoTrac, find information on one case in which technology is used for sexual voyeurism or exhibitionism. Examples might include reality TV or JenniCam, the student who let Web site visitors visually into her dorm room via a Webcam. Using the example, discuss the following:

  a. Do you think technology changes the nature of the relationship between exhibitor and viewer? If so, how?

  b. How does technologically mediated sexual display compare to other kinds of sexual shows and consumption?

  c. Do you think more people are likely to consume this type of media because they can do so anonymously?

5. *Meaning and Atypical Sexual Behavior*

Using InfoTrac, search the following terms to clarify the difference between

- **Cross-dressing**
- **Transvestism**
- **Female Impersonator**
- **Transsexual**

Define each term in distinction to the others. Then give one example of cases from the news or the media for each term. For example, can you think of a popular sports or film star that cross-dresses? A film that involves a man dressed as a woman? A well-known transsexual who has written about his / her experience?

6. *Autoerotic Asphyxiation: Reading Case Studies*

Using InfoTrac, locate the article entitled "Autoerotic Asphyxia: The Development of a Paraphilia" in *Journal of the American Academy of Child and Adolescent Psychiatry,* September 1994. Read the article and then answer the following questions:

a.   What are the main features of autoerotic asphyxia?

b.   Who is most likely to engage in this behavior? And under what circumstances?

c.   Do you feel a case study approach was effective in this research?

d.   What were common factors across each of the cases?

e.   What additional questions do you have about autoerotic asphyxiation?

7. *Sexual Power Plays*

Search InfoTrac to find studies of **sadomasochistic behavior** and **bondage**. Review the related articles, and then address the following questions:

a.   The figure of leather-clad, whip-wielding dominatrix is a well-known, and sometimes comic, image. Who is likely to seek out the services of a dominatrix? Why is this figure considered erotic? Why is she considered funny?

b.   Is there any evidence that consensual sadomasochistic sexual behaviors have any relation to experiences of sexual violence or abuse? Why or why not?

c.	Do you think sex always involves some sort of power play? In other words, is one person likely to be dominant and the other submissive? Why or why not?

## 8.	Sadomasochism: Reading the Research

Use InfoTrac to locate the following two articles:

"Investigating the Underlying Structure in Sadomasochistically Oriented Behavior" in *Archives of Sexual Behavior*, April 2002.

"The PLEASURE of the PAIN: Why Some People Need S & M" in *Psychology Today*, September 1999.

After reading the two articles, answer the following questions:

a.	What is sadomasochistic behavior? How did each of the articles define sadomasochistic behavior?

b.	How did each article approach understanding sadomasochistic behaviors?

c.	What more would you like to know about sadomasochistic behavior?

d.	Do you feel that sadomasochistic behavior is atypical sexual behavior? Why or why not?

## 9.	Gender and Atypical Sexual Behaviors

Using InfoTrac, learn more about atypical sexual behaviors. Consider the following topics and then answer the questions below:

- **Paraphilia**
- **Voyeurism**
- **Exhibitionism**
- **Zoophilia**
- **Frotteurism**
- **Necrophilia**

a.	How common are these behaviors? Does the incidence differ across gender?

b.	Are different treatments equally effective for each?

10.   Fetishes

Using InfoTrac conduct two searches using the key term **fetish**. Conduct the first search surveying all available sources and the second limiting the search to only referred publications. Compare the results from each search and answer the following:

a.   Consider the results across the two searches: How is the term "fetish" being used? Is there a difference in the way the term is used in the context of research versus the mainstream use of the word?

b.   Consider the results across the two searches: What objects or body parts are included in the discussion of fetishes? Do these differ across the two sources of information?

c.   Some fetishes focus on an isolated body part (i.e., feet). U.S. culture emphasizes a sexualized portrayal of women's breasts. Could an individual's focus on women's breasts as a source of sexual arousal be classified as a fetish? Why or why not?

11.   Zoophilia: A Research Study

Using InfoTrac, locate the article entitled "Zoophilia in Men: A Study of Sexual Interest in Animals" in *Archives of Sexual Behavior*, December 2003.

Read the article and then answer the following questions:

a.   Has zoophilia been the topic of much scientific research? Why or why not?

b.   Who is most likely to engage in this behavior? And under what circumstances?

c.   How were the data for this research collected? Do you feel that this is a reliable way to collect accurate data on the topic? Why or why not?

d.   What does this study add to the understanding of zoophilia? What questions do you still have on the topic?

Chapter 19

Sexual Coercion

1.   *Rape and Culture*

Sex by force or under threat of violence can be perpetrated by a person known to you or a stranger. Victims include women, men, and children; most, but not all, perpetrators are men.

Why does rape occur? And why does the United States have such a high incidence of rape? Some have called our society a "rape culture." What do you think?

Using InfoTrac, examine recent research on **rape and culture**. Use the articles to find one aspect of U.S. culture that you think contributes to the problem. This could be the media, gender inequality, machismo in the culture, or any other topic you think relevant.

Write a brief discussion that includes the following:

      a.   How does your topic contribute to a rape culture?

      b.   Is there evidence that it affects male and female sexual behavior?

      c.   Have there been efforts to change or modify this cultural element?

      d.   Do you think the cultural issue you chose can be changed to help end violence towards women (or men)?

  BONUS: What would evolutionary psychologists such as Randy Thornhill and Craig Palmer say about the notion that rates of rape are related to the qualities of a culture? Outline their perspective and the evidence for it and contrast to the cultural argument above. Which view do you support?

2. *The Language of Rape: Victim vs. Survivor*

Using InfoTrac, search the key terms **rape, rape victim**, and **rape survivor.** Review the search results and then answer the following:

    a.   What images accompany the use of the terms "rape victim" and "rape survivor?" Who is likely to use each term?

    b.   What type of research is currently being done to understand rape? What are the different approaches being used? Is there a difference in the rape language or terminology used across these approaches?

    c.   What type of research is being done to understand why rape occurs? Which explanations focus on the behaviors of the rape victim and which explanations focus on the behaviors of the perpetrator?

3. *Rape as a Weapon of War*

Explore the role sexual violence plays in war. Using InfoTrac, search **rape** and the name of a region of conflict in the world, past or present. Then answer the following questions:

    a.   Who were the perpetrators of rape? Who were the victims?

    b.   Were the rapes organized by one of the parties in the conflict or were they individual cases?

    c.   Do survivors tend to report the rape? If so, to whom?

    d.   Has there been legal follow-up to punish the perpetrators?

    e.   How have survivors adjusted since the fighting ended? Do you see rape as a weapon of war? Was rape particularly meaningful because of local gender roles, religious conflict, or ethnic factors?

    BONUS: Write about the international efforts to have rape understood and prosecuted as a war crime.

4.   *Sexual Assault in Prison*

The problem of **prison rape** only began to receive public attention in the last few years. However, hundreds of thousands of rapes occur in prison annually. The victims are both women and men. Sexual violence plays an important role in the social structure of prisons where the less powerful may be controlled by more powerful inmates or guards.

Using InfoTrac, search for information about prison rape and then answer the following:

a.   Why do you think this problem was overlooked for so long?

b.   Give an example of a joke or other lighthearted reference in popular culture to rapes of men in prison. Why do you think it has not been taken seriously?

c.   What role does the AIDS epidemic play in the new attention to this problem?

d.   Do you think that recognizing male-on-male prison rape will help gain attention for men as rape victims in general? Why or why not?

5.   *Child Sexual Abuse*

Use InfoTrac to evaluate each of the following measures as ways to reduce rates of sexual abuse in childhood. (You may need to try more than one search term.)

- **Meghan's Law**
- **Sex education beginning in elementary school**
- **Censorship of films and books with children and sex (Lolita, for example)**
- **Strict control of pedophile sites on the Internet**
- **Access to divorce**
- **Teaching children not to touch others**

Are all of these good ideas or not? Write a brief essay that deals with each topic and addresses the following questions:

a.   Which measures contribute to child sex abuse?

b.   Which measures may help prevent child sex abuse?

c.   Of the useful measures, would they also help to prevent incest or does that require a different approach? If so, why?

6. *Falsely Accused: Victims and Perpetrators*

Using InfoTrac, search for recent data on the number of rapes reported, estimates of unreported rapes, and the number of cases where an alleged perpetrator claims he / she has been falsely accused. Then consider the following:

    a.   Why is it important to hear the cases of those who claim to have been falsely accused?

    b.   Name at least one case in U.S. history where men who were falsely accused of rape were executed. Describe the circumstances.

    c.   Describe a case where a victim of rape was not believed (though the story was later proven to have occurred)? Describe one case of false accusation.

    d.   What role can DNA evidence play in the legal processing of rape cases? What circumstances might lead to DNA evidence not being obtained?

7. *Rape and Power*

What do date **rape drugs** such as **Rophypnol** indicate about power relations in sexual violence? The so-called date rape drugs render a person completely passive. Aside from their potential health effects, they make the victim completely unresponsive so that he or she can be sexually abused.

Using InfoTrac, find and briefly describe one case where a woman or man was sought out for sex expressly because they were unconscious or unresponsive. This might include hospital patients or even a corpse.

What does this case suggest about the perpetrator's view of sexual partnership?

8. *The Human Cost of Rape*

Using InfoTrac, search a variety of reports about the effect of rape both on the survivor and on the well being of society as a whole. Then make a list of the psychological and physical health effects, effects on behavior, and cultural effects rape continues to have.

Continue the following list:
        Feelings of low self-esteem
        Fear of rape
        A fear many women have about venturing out at night

9.   *Rape and Your Campus Community*

Rape and **date rape** often take place on college campuses. Most campuses are paying attention to this issue by having educational meetings at dorms, sororities, fraternities, and other groups. To find out the answer to some of the questions listed below you may need to contact student services, campus police, or the student health service on your campus.

a.   Have there been any incidents of rape reported on your campus in the last year? In the last five years?

b.   Was there an investigation of the incident? What was the outcome? Was the person caught?

c.   How was the incident communicated to the campus community?

d.   Have there been any incidents of date rape on your campus reported in the last year? In the last five years?

e.   Was there an investigation of the incident? What was the outcome? Was the person caught?

f.   How are incidents of rape and date rape handled similarly or differently on campus? Are they communicated to the campus community in similar or different ways?

g.   Were there any rape incidents related to specific groups such as athletes or fraternities? Were there any rape incidents involving alcohol or other drugs?

h.   What services are available for people who have been victims of rape at school or other places? List both school and community resources.

Using InfoTrac, locate articles about **campus rape** and **date rape**.

Write a brief summary of how your investigation of rape at your campus community is similar to or different from what is reflected in the research literature.

10. Sexual Harassment

Sexual harassment is not just something that gets the attention of the EEOC or the nightly news. Most of us have either experienced it firsthand or seen it occur – maybe we have even been harassers ourselves.

Most cases go unreported. Describe a case that you observed or experienced. Pick a case of either an unwanted advance or a hostile or offensive environment in a work, school, or other institutional setting. How did it affect the personal and work life of the person who was harassed? Was anything done about it?

Then, using InfoTrac, find an example of a case or an article that discusses a similar instance or circumstance to the one you described.

How do you think the type of problem you described should be addressed? Legal recourse that leads to punishment for the perpetrator? Education for that person? What other strategies might lessen the incidence of sexual harassment?

11. Sexual Harassment and the Campus Community

College campuses are not immune from incidents of sexual harassment. To find out the answer to some of the questions listed below you may need to contact student services, campus police, or the student health service on your campus.

a. Have there been any incidents of sexual harassment reported on your campus in the last year? In the last five years?

b. Was there an investigation of the incident? What was the outcome? Was the person caught?

c. How was it communicated to the campus community?

d. What services are available for people who have been victims of sexual harassment at school or other places? List both school and community resources.

Using InfoTrac, locate articles about **sexual harassment on campus**.

Write a brief summary of how your investigation of sexual harassment at your campus community is similar to or different from what is reflected in the research literature.

Chapter 20

Sex for Sale

1. Erotica vs. Pornography

Supreme Court Justice Stewart Potter once said that obscenity is hard to define but "I know it when I see it." Who is to judge what is obscene? Using InfoTrac, write a definition for each that distinguishes between the following two terms:

- **Pornography**
- **Erotica**

Do you think that there is a significant distinction between the two? Explain. Then discuss the following:

a.   In what medium (Internet? TV?) is pornography more prevalent? In which do you find most erotica? Why is there a difference?

b.   Most sexually explicit materials are designed for men, both gay and straight. Is there erotica for women? Is there pornography for women? Explain your answer and provide examples.

c.   Do you think sexually explicit materials can be valuable for their contribution to sexuality? Do you think sexually explicit materials can be valuable for their creative and political value (free speech)? Explain your answer.

2. Pornography, Obscenity, and Free Speech

Using InfoTrac, explore one of the following cases or institutions and examine the struggle between those who want to control **pornography** and those who maintain it is protected by the right of **free speech** under the First Amendment of the U.S. Constitution.

- **U.S. Supreme Court / U.S. Congress**
- **Henry Miller**
- **Comstock Laws**
- **Playboy**
- **Larry Flynt and Hustler**
- **The Children's Internet Protection Act**
- **Janet Jackson and Super Bowl 2004**
- **Howard Stern**

3. Pornography on the Web

"The most successful Internet-related business is the sex business," said *Computer World* magazine in 1997. Pornography on the Internet is estimated to be a $2 billion-a-year business today and growing.

Using InfoTrac, explore the proliferation of sex on the Web. Then discuss the following:

    a.   Why has the Internet become such an important medium for the distribution of pornography? (Hint: What do the Internet and home VCRs have in common?)

    b.   Do you think that access to pornography on the Web should be protected as a right of privacy? What about using the Internet at school, work, or in a public library to peruse porn sites? What can supervisors of those computers do to prevent porn site surfing?

    BONUS: As authorities regulate the Web, pornographers find new technologies or new ways to use old technologies. Can you think of ways they might do this? Do you think trying to control pornography is impossible?

4. Child Pornography

Child pornography is a booming international trade that has been aided by the Web. Using InfoTrac, read about some of the efforts to stop the flow of children's images for sexual consumption. Write about one of the following themes:

    a.   The use of both real and computer-generated virtual depictions of children in sexual poses. Is there a difference? Is the virtual image less harmful because it involves no real child?

    b.   The **V-chip**, introduced to keep kids away from obscene Web sites. What are parents and Internet service providers doing to prevent children from being contacted by pedophiles through chat rooms?

5.   *Pornography as International Big Business*

The global traffic in pornography nets some $8 billion a year. Using InfoTrac, read about how both pornographers and legitimate businesses profit from sexually explicit materials. Use search terms **Internet, business, pornography**.

Make a list of the types of legitimate businesses that indirectly gain from being conduits of pornographic traffic. (Think of how customers pay for pornography, where they view pornography, how it is delivered to them, etc.)

Have these businesses made efforts to end their role as providers of pornography?

BONUS: Is there pornography available in your neighborhood? List the various places where sexually explicit materials are on sale or for rent.

6.   *Who Reads Playboy?*

Using InfoTrac, locate an article entitled "What Sort of Man Reads *Playboy*?: The Self-Reported Influence of *Playboy* on the Construction of Masculinity" in *The Journal of Men's Studies*, Winter 2003. Read the article and then answer the following questions:

a.   What was the purpose and method of the study?

b.   How were participants located? Do you think they are representative of the *Playboy* readership? Why or why not?

c.   What do you think was the most surprising finding of the study?

d.   How did participants describe their first *Playboy* experience?

e.   What did participants' *Playboy* experiences reflect regarding their ideas about masculinity?

f.   How did participants describe their thinking about women?

g.   What did the authors ultimately conclude about their findings?

7. *College Experience of Pornography and Explicit Materials*

Using InfoTrac, locate the following two articles:

"Reactions to Pornography on a College Campus: For or Against?" in *Sex Roles: A Journal of Research*, July 1993.

"Searching for Sexually Explicit Materials on the Internet: An Exploratory Study of College Students' Behavior and Attitudes" in *Archives of Sexual Behavior*, April 2001.

Read the articles and answer the following questions:

a. According to these articles, what are the attitudes that college students tend to have regarding pornography? How does each of the articles support this?

b. How are college students' attitudes about pornography similar to or different from the larger population? Why do you think this is?

c. How common is it for college students to access pornographic material via the Internet?

d. How are the attitudes and behaviors of female college students similar to or different from male college students?

e. Do you think consumption of pornography in college populations is a concern? Why or why not?

8.   *Prostitution*

Prostitution is the exchange of sexual services for money or other valuables. It takes many forms. Using InfoTrac, answer one of the following:

a.   Do you think all women who work as prostitutes are exploited? Why or why not? Compare the circumstances of women who are in some way coerced into performing sex work and those who enter it on their own terms. What do those women share in common, if anything? Compare organizations against prostitution with those such as COYOTE.

b.   How do male prostitutes differ from female? What aspects of their working situation tend to be different from that of women?

c.   Anyone who is a sex worker is potentially exposed to HIV and other infectious diseases. Examine the efforts of world health organizations to prevent STDs among sex workers. Describe one program that has had success and explain why.

9.   *Child Prostitution*

Children are prostituted in the United States and around the world. They may be prostitutes for sex "tourists" in Thailand, for soldiers in areas of armed conflict, or wherever poverty creates armies of street children who have no other means of support. Some are sold into sexual slavery by their impoverished parents.

Using InfoTrac, examine the state of **child prostitution** in one particular region of the world. Describe the following:

a.   How common is child prostitution?

b.   Who are the most vulnerable children?

c.   Why are children more susceptible to STDs than adults?

d.   Who is exploiting the children (their "pimp")? Who profits?

e.   Who are their sexual "clients"?

f.   What are international organizations or governmental agencies doing to help them?